Better Homes & Gardens®

Hometown

FAVORITES

Delicious Down-Home Recipes

Volume II

Meredith® Consumer Marketing

Des Moines, Iowa

Better Homes & Gardens®

Hometown Favorites

MEREDITH CONSUMER MARKETING
Director of Direct Marketing-Books: Daniel Fagan
Marketing Operations Manager: Max Daily
Assistant Marketing Manager: Kylie Dazzo
Business Manager: Diane Umland
Senior Production Manager: Al Rodruck

WATERBURY PUBLICATIONS, INC.
Editorial Director: Lisa Kingsley
Associate Editor: Tricia Bergman
Creative Director: Ken Carlson
Associate Design Director: Doug Samuelson
Production Assistant: Mindy Samuelson
Contributing Copy Editors: Terri Fredrickson, Peg Smith
Contributing Indexer: Mary Williams

***BETTER HOMES & GARDENS®* MAGAZINE**
Editor in Chief: Stephen Orr
Editors: Nancy Wall Hopkins, Jan Miller

MEREDITH CORPORATION
Executive Chairman: Stephen M. Lacy

In Memoriam: E.T. Meredith III (1933–2003)

Our seal assures you that every recipe in *Hometown Favorites* has been tested in the Better Homes & Gardens® Test Kitchen. This means that each recipe is practical and reliable, and it meets our high standards of taste appeal. We guarantee your satisfaction with this book for as long as you own it.

All of us at Meredith Consumer Marketing are dedicated to providing you with information and ideas to enhance your home. We welcome your comments and suggestions. Write to us at: Meredith Consumer Marketing, 1716 Locust St, Des Moines, IA 50309-3023.

Pictured on front cover: Cinnamon Roll-Apple Pie Bake, page 171

Contents

CHAPTER 1

Appetizers

Whether you're bringing a dish to a party or hosting a party yourself, this selection of nibbles, dips, spreads, sliders, and drinks offers up fare for celebrating.

8

21

27

Seasoned Pepitas and Peanuts

This crunchy, nutty, nicely spiced (not hot!) combo is absolutely addictive. Bake a batch for a party or simply to have on hand as a healthy snack. Store at room temperature in a tightly sealed container.

1. Preheat oven to 350°F. In a small bowl combine first seven ingredients (through coriander). Spread pumpkin seeds and peanuts in a 15×10-inch baking pan. Drizzle with butter mixture; toss to coat.

2. Bake 10 to 12 minutes or until lightly toasted, stirring once. Cool.

FOR 32 SERVINGS Use two 15×10-inch baking pans.

PER SERVING *117 cal., 10 g fat (2 g sat. fat), 4 mg chol., 92 mg sodium, 3 g carb., 2 g fiber, 5 g pro.*

PREP 15 minutes
BAKE 10 minutes

16 servings	ingredients	32 servings
2 Tbsp.	butter, melted	¼ cup
1 Tbsp.	packed brown sugar	2 Tbsp.
1½ tsp.	chili powder	1 Tbsp.
1 tsp.	dried oregano, crushed	2 tsp.
½ tsp.	salt	1 tsp.
½ tsp.	ground cumin	1 tsp.
½ tsp.	ground coriander	1 tsp.
1 cup	pumpkin seeds (pepitas)	2 cups
1 cup	raw peanuts or Spanish-style peanuts	2 cups

Fired-Up Almonds

Ground chipotle chile gives these sweet and spicy snack nuts a rich, smoky flavor. A generous dose of brown sugar caramelizes in the oven and creates a delightfully crunchy candied crust.

1. Preheat oven to 350°F. Line a 15×10-inch baking pan with foil.

2. In a large bowl whisk egg white until foamy. Add almonds; toss to coat. Stir in remaining ingredients. Spread nuts in prepared pan.

3. Bake 25 to 30 minutes or until nuts are toasted and appear dry, stirring twice. Remove from oven; stir again. Cool. Break up any large clusters.

FOR 24 SERVINGS Use two 15×10-inch baking pans.

PER SERVING *233 cal., 18 g fat (1 g sat. fat), 0 mg chol., 100 mg sodium, 14 g carb., 5 g fiber, 8 g pro.*

PREP 10 minutes
BAKE 25 minutes

12 servings	ingredients	24 servings
1	egg white	2
3 cups	whole almonds	6 cups
⅓ cup	packed brown sugar	⅔ cup
1 tsp.	kosher salt	2 tsp.
1 tsp.	ground cumin	2 tsp.
½ tsp.	ground chipotle chile pepper or cayenne pepper	1 tsp.
⅛ tsp.	ground cinnamon	¼ tsp.

Rosemary-Orange Marinated Olives

A quartet of Mediterranean ingredients—garlic, rosemary, fresh orange, and toasted fennel seeds—gives these elegant Greek cocktail olives fresh and complex flavor.

1. Rinse olives and pat dry; place in a medium bowl. Add two of the rosemary sprigs and the remaining ingredients; toss together. Cover and chill 24 to 48 hours, tossing once or twice.

2. Let stand at room temperature 1 hour before serving. Transfer to a serving bowl, replacing the 2 rosemary sprigs with the remaining fresh sprig for garnish.

*TIP In a dry skillet toast small amounts of nuts, seeds, or spices over medium heat 3 to 5 minutes, stirring frequently.

FOR 20 SERVINGS In Step 1, add four rosemary sprigs.

PER SERVING *94 cal., 10 g fat (1 g sat. fat), 0 mg chol., 420 mg sodium, 0 g carb., 0 g fiber, 0 g pro.*

PREP 15 minutes
CHILL 24 hours

10 servings	ingredients	20 servings
2 cups	brine-cured Kalamata olives	4 cups
3	sprigs fresh rosemary	6
¼ cup	extra-virgin olive oil	½ cup
2	large cloves garlic, lightly crushed	4
2	wide strips orange zest, sliced in thin julienne pieces	4
½ tsp.	fennel seeds, toasted* and crushed	1 tsp.

Roasted Red Pepper and Feta Dip

Roasting the peppers before coarsely pureeing sweetens them and imparts them with a pleasantly smoky flavor. To please both carb lovers and carb avoiders, serve the dip with pita chips and cut-up vegetables.

1. Preheat oven to 425°F. Line a baking sheet with foil. Cut sweet peppers in half. Remove and discard stems, seeds, and membranes. Place pepper halves, cut sides down, on the prepared baking sheet. Add onion wedges and garlic to the baking sheet. Brush vegetables and garlic with some olive oil.

2. Roast 30 to 35 minutes or until pepper skins are blistered and onion and garlic are tender. Wrap foil around vegetables. Let stand 15 minutes. Carefully open foil. Peel and discard skins from peppers.

3. Place peppers and onion in a food processor. Squeeze garlic into food processor. Add remaining olive oil and the next five ingredients (through crushed red pepper). Cover and pulse until nearly smooth, scraping sides occasionally.

4. Transfer dip to a serving bowl. If desired, top with additional oregano. Serve dip with pita chips and/or vegetables.

*TIP Or for 6 servings substitute 1 cup purchased roasted red sweet peppers, drained, for the two fresh sweet peppers. Roast onions and garlic as directed. For 12 servings, use 2 cups purchased roasted red sweet peppers, drained.

FOR 12 SERVINGS In Step 1, line two baking sheets with foil.

PER SERVING *118 cal., 9 g fat (3 g sat. fat), 17 mg chol., 223 mg sodium, 7 g carb., 1 g fiber, 4 g pro.*

PREP 25 minutes
ROAST 30 minutes **STAND** 15 minutes

6 servings	ingredients	12 servings
2	red sweet peppers*	4
1	onion, cut into ½-inch wedges	2
4	cloves garlic (unpeeled)	8
2 Tbsp.	olive oil	¼ cup
1 cup	crumbled feta cheese	2 cups
2 Tbsp.	lemon juice	¼ cup
2 Tbsp.	fresh oregano leaves	¼ cup
¼ tsp.	kosher salt	½ tsp.
⅛ to ¼ tsp.	crushed red pepper	¼ to ½ tsp.
	Pita chips or cut-up vegetables	

Caramelized Onion Dip

With ribbons of onions slowly cooked with a little sugar to maximize their natural sweetness, this perfect party dip raises the bar on the version made with dry French onion soup mix.

PREP 20 minutes   **COOK** 15 minutes
CHILL 1 hour   **STAND** 20 minutes

8 servings	ingredients	16 servings
2 Tbsp.	olive oil	¼ cup
2 cups	chopped green onions	4 cups
2 tsp.	sugar	4 tsp.
1 tsp.	salt	2 tsp.
4	cloves garlic, minced	8
1½ cups	light sour cream	3 cups
⅔ cup	light mayonnaise	1⅓ cups
¼ tsp.	black pepper	½ tsp.
	Chopped chives (optional)	
	Thick-cut vegetable chips or potato chips, and/or cut-up raw vegetables	

1. In large skillet heat oil over medium heat. Add onions, sugar, and half the salt; toss. Reduce heat to medium-low. Cook and stir 15 to 20 minutes or until onions are golden. Remove from heat; cool. Stir in garlic.

2. In a medium bowl combine the cooled onion mixture, sour cream, mayonnaise, remaining salt, and pepper. Transfer to a serving bowl. Cover with plastic wrap; chill 1 hour to blend flavors.

3. Stir dip; let stand 20 minutes at room temperature before serving. If desired, sprinkle with chives. Serve with chips or raw vegetables.

PER SERVING *150 cal., 12 g fat (4 g sat. fat), 16 mg chol., 467 mg sodium, 10 g carb., 1 g fiber, 2 g pro.*

Shrimp and Olive Dip

Cream cheese spread with jalapeño serves as a base for this Mexican-inspired dip. Make it at least 1 hour ahead to allow the flavors to blend.

1. Thaw shrimp, if frozen. In a medium skillet melt butter over medium heat. Add shrimp; cook and stir 3 to 4 minutes or until opaque. Chop shrimp.

2. In a large bowl beat cream cheese spread, sour cream, garlic salt, and cumin with a mixer on medium until combined. Beat in sweet pepper, green onions, olives, half the cheese, and half the cilantro on low just until combined. Stir in shrimp. Transfer to a serving bowl. Cover with plastic wrap; chill 1 hour to blend flavors.

3. Gently stir dip before serving. Top with remaining cheese and cilantro. Serve with cucumber slices, chips, or baguette slices.

PER SERVING *84 cal., 6 g fat (3 g sat. fat), 46 mg chol., 208 mg sodium, 3 g carb., 0 g fiber, 5 g pro.*

PREP 25 minutes
CHILL 1 hour

12 servings	ingredients	24 servings
8 oz.	fresh or frozen medium peeled and deveined medium shrimp	1 lb.
2 tsp.	butter	4 tsp.
one 7.5-oz. container	cream cheese spread with jalapeño, softened	two 7.5-oz. containers
⅓ cup	sour cream	⅔ cup
½ tsp.	garlic salt	1 tsp.
½ tsp.	ground cumin	1 tsp.
½ cup	finely chopped red sweet pepper	1 cup
⅓ cup	chopped green onions	⅔ cup
⅓ cup	chopped pitted ripe olives	⅔ cup
⅓ cup	crumbled queso blanco, queso fresco, or feta cheese	⅔ cup
1 Tbsp.	snipped fresh cilantro	2 Tbsp.
	Cucumber slices, tortilla chips, or toasted baguette slices	

Jack Cheese and Smoky Chipotle Fondue

A Swiss classic gets a Tex-Mex makeover in this warm and cheesy fondue flavored with Monterey Jack cheese and smoky chipotle chiles in adobo sauce.

PREP 30 minutes
COOK 20 minutes

16 servings	ingredients	32 servings
4 slices	bacon, halved crosswise	8 slices
¼ cup	finely chopped green onions	½ cup
¼ cup	finely chopped red or yellow sweet pepper	½ cup
2	cloves garlic, minced	4
2 tsp.	all-purpose flour	4 tsp.
4 cups	shredded Monterey Jack cheese	8 cups
one 16 oz. carton	sour cream	two 16 oz. cartons
2 to 3 tsp.	finely chopped chipotle peppers in adobo sauce	4 to 6 tsp.
	French or Italian bread cubes and/or tortilla chips	

1. In a heavy saucepan cook bacon until crisp. Drain bacon on paper towels; reserve 1 Tbsp. drippings in pan.

2. Add green onions, sweet pepper, and garlic to saucepan. Cook and stir over medium heat 5 minutes or until vegetables are tender. Stir in flour. Stir in cheese, sour cream, and chipotle peppers. Cook and stir over medium-low heat until cheese is melted and mixture is slightly thickened. Crumble bacon.

3. Transfer cheese mixture to fondue pot. Top with crumbled bacon. Keep warm up to 2 hours. Serve with bread cubes and/or tortilla chips.

FOR 32 SERVINGS In Step 1, reserve 2 Tbsp. pan drippings.

PER SERVING *186 cal., 16 g fat (10 g sat. fat), 40 mg chol., 200 mg sodium, 2 g carb., 0 g fiber, 8 g pro.*

Melted Tiny Tomatoes

Roasting softens the tomatoes to the point that they can be slathered on crusty bread. Make this garden-fresh appetizer at the height of tomato season, when the fruits are at their sweetest, juiciest, and ripest.

1. Preheat oven to 400°F. Place tomatoes in a shallow baking dish. Drizzle with oil. Stir to coat. Sprinkle with chili powder, sugar, and salt.

2. Roast, uncovered, 12 to 15 minutes, or just until skins start to burst, gently stirring once halfway through roasting time. Serve warm with crusty bread.

PER SERVING *39 cal., 3 g fat (0 g sat. fat), 0 mg chol., 75 mg sodium, 3 g carb., 1 g fiber, 1 g pro.*

START TO FINISH 20 minutes

10 servings	ingredients	20 servings
4 cups	assorted tiny tomatoes	8 cups
2 Tbsp.	olive oil	4 Tbsp.
2 tsp.	chili powder	4 tsp.
½ tsp.	sugar	1 tsp.
½ tsp.	kosher salt	1 tsp.
	Crusty bread	

Grilled Stuffed Pepper Poppers

Who doesn't love a grilled pepper stuffed with warm and gooey cheese? Use a mix of jalapeños and mini sweet peppers to please all palates.

1. In a bowl beat cream cheese with a mixer on low to medium until smooth. Beat in Cotija, thyme, garlic, and chipotle pepper. Stir in nuts.

2. Cut a lengthwise slit in one side of each fresh pepper to create a pocket, being careful not to cut the pepper in half. Leave stem intact and remove the seeds and membranes. Using a small spoon, fill each pepper with some of the cheese mixture.

3. Prepare grill** for indirect heat. Place filled peppers in a greased grill basket or on a greased vegetable grilling pan. Cover and grill 5 to 10 minutes or until peppers are soft and filling is heated through.

*TIP Chile peppers contain oils that can burn your skin and eyes. When working with them, wear plastic or rubber gloves. If your bare hands touch the peppers, wash with soap and warm water.

**OVEN DIRECTIONS Preheat oven to 425°F. Place filled peppers in a shallow baking dish. Bake 10 to 15 minutes or until peppers are soft and filling is heated through.

PER SERVING *71 cal., 6 g fat (3 g sat. fat), 15 mg chol., 92 mg sodium, 2 g carb., 0 g fiber, 2 g pro.*

PREP 30 minutes
GRILL 5 minutes

10 servings	ingredients	20 servings
½	8-oz. pkg. cream cheese, softened	1
⅓ cup	crumbled Cotija or queso fresco	⅔ cup
1 Tbsp.	snipped fresh thyme	2 Tbsp.
1	clove garlic, minced	2
¼ to ½ tsp.	ground chipotle chile pepper or Spanish paprika	½ to 1 tsp.
2 to 3 Tbsp.	pine nuts or pecans, chopped and toasted (tip, page 8)	4 to 6 Tbsp.
10 to 12	jalapeños* and/or miniature red and yellow sweet peppers	20 to 24

Chicken-Feta Phyllo Cups with Tzatziki Sauce

These crunchy pastry cups filled with a colorful mixture of chicken, cheese, vegetables, olives, and herbs are little fussy to make, but are sure to impress even the most sophisticated party guest.

PREP 45 minutes

BAKE 10 minutes   **COOL** 5 minutes

6 servings	ingredients	12 servings
	Nonstick cooking spray	
8	sheets frozen phyllo dough, thawed	16
¾ cup	boiling water	1½ cups
⅔ cup	whole wheat couscous	1⅓ cups
2 cups	chopped cooked chicken breast	4 cups
1 cup	chopped fresh spinach	2 cups
½ cup	roasted red sweet pepper, drained and chopped	1 cup
⅓ cup	crumbled reduced-fat feta cheese	⅔ cup
¼ cup	finely chopped, pitted Kalamata olives	½ cup
¼ cup	bottled light Italian salad dressing	½ cup
1 cup	plain low-fat Greek or regular yogurt	2 cups
½ cup	finely chopped seeded cucumber	1 cup
2 Tbsp.	snipped fresh mint	4 Tbsp.
⅛ tsp.	salt	¼ tsp.
	lemon wedges (optional)	

1. Preheat oven to 350°F. Lightly coat twelve 2½-inch muffin cups with cooking spray. On a work surface, lightly coat one sheet of phyllo dough with cooking spray (keep remaining phyllo covered with plastic wrap to prevent it from drying out). Top with another sheet of phyllo and lightly coat with cooking spray. Repeat layering twice, making a stack of four phyllo sheets. Repeat with remaining phyllo and additional cooking spray to make a second stack.

2. Cut each stack in half lengthwise; cut crosswise into thirds. Press rectangles into prepared muffin cups, pleating to fit. Bake 5 minutes or just until phyllo starts to brown.

3. Meanwhile, in a large bowl combine boiling water and couscous; cover and let stand 5 minutes. Fluff with a fork. Stir in the next six ingredients (through salad dressing).

4. Spoon chicken mixture into partially baked phyllo cups. Bake 5 to 7 minutes or until heated through and phyllo is golden. Cool in muffin cups on a wire rack 5 minutes. Remove from muffin cups.

5. For the Tzatziki Sauce, in a bowl stir together yogurt, cucumber, mint, and salt. Serve sauce with Chicken-Feta Phyllo Cups and, if desired, lemon wedges.

FOR 12 SERVINGS Use two 12 cup muffin pans. In Step 1, make four stacks of phyllo.

PER SERVING *288 cal., 8 g fat (2 g sat. fat), 46 mg chol., 528 mg sodium, 31 g carb., 2 g fiber, 24 g pro.*

Beef Nachos

Double the recipe when you're hosting a big crowd to watch The Big Game. Serve different salsas— red, green, hot, medium, and mild to accommodate every taste.

1. Preheat broiler. In a large skillet cook ground beef over medium heat until browned, breaking up any large pieces. Drain off fat. Stir in beans, salt, and pepper. Heat through. Remove from heat; cover and set aside.

2. Meanwhile, set aside 2 Tbsp. each green onions and cilantro. For salsa, in a blender combine tomatoes, remaining green onions, cilantro, chili powder, garlic powder, and cumin. Blend until smooth. Set aside.

3. On a baking sheet arrange chips in a single layer. Sprinkle with cheese. Broil 5 to 6 inches from heat 2 to 3 minutes or until cheese is melted. Top with ground beef mixture and about half the salsa. Broil 2 to 3 minutes or until heated through. Top with reserved onion and cilantro. Serve with remaining salsa.

FOR 8 SERVINGS In Step 2, set aside ¼ cup each green onions and cilantro.

PER SERVING *471 cal., 26 g fat (11 g sat. fat), 86 mg chol., 1,019 mg sodium, 31 g carb., 6 g fiber, 29 g pro.*

PREP 15 minutes
COOK 10 minutes **BROIL** 4 minutes

4 servings	ingredients	8 servings
12 oz.	ground beef	24 oz.
1 cup	canned kidney beans, rinsed and drained	2 cups
½ tsp.	salt	1 tsp.
½ tsp.	black pepper	1 tsp.
1	bunch green onions, sliced	2
⅔ cup	coarsely chopped fresh cilantro	1⅓ cups
one 14.5-oz. can	fire-roasted tomatoes, undrained	two 14.5-oz. cans
2 tsp.	chili powder	4 tsp.
1½ tsp.	garlic powder	1 Tbsp.
1 tsp.	ground cumin	2 tsp.
4 cups	corn tortilla chips	8 cups
1 cup	shredded cheddar cheese	2 cups

Prosciutto-Wrapped Honey-Lemon Shrimp

Honey and lemon juice create a sweet and glossy glaze on these tender shrimp swaddled in crispy prosciutto. They're best served warm but are nearly as good at room temperature.

8 servings	ingredients	16 servings
24 (about 1 lb.)	fresh or frozen jumbo shrimp in shells	48 (about 2 lb.)
1	lemon	2
2 Tbsp.	honey	4 Tbsp.
2 tsp.	snipped fresh parsley	4 tsp.
4 to 5 oz.	very thinly sliced prosciutto	8 to 10 oz.

1. Thaw shrimp, if frozen. Preheat broiler. Peel and devein shrimp, leaving tails intact. Rinse shrimp; pat dry with paper towels. Place shrimp in a large bowl. Remove ½ tsp. zest and 2 Tbsp. juice from lemon. In a small bowl combine lemon zest and juice, honey, and parsley. Pour over shrimp; toss gently to coat.

2. Cut prosciutto slices in half crosswise then in half lengthwise (24 pieces total for 8 servings; 48 pieces for 16 servings). Wrap a piece of prosciutto around each shrimp; secure with a wooden pick.

3. Place shrimp on the lightly greased unheated rack of a broiler pan. Broil 4 to 5 inches from the heat 4 to 6 minutes or until shrimp are opaque and prosciutto is crisp, turning once.

4. If desired, sprinkle shrimp with additional lemon zest and snipped fresh parsley and serve with additional honey for dipping.

FOR 16 SERVINGS In Step 1, remove 1 tsp. zest and ¼ cup juice from lemons. In Step 3, broil shrimp in batches.

PER SERVING *84 cal., 4 g fat (0 g sat. fat), 32 mg chol., 283 mg sodium, 5 g carb., 0 g fiber, 8 g pro.*

Salami, Cheese, and Pepper Sandwich Loaf

Tote this hearty loaf—tightly wrapped in plastic and in a cooler—to your next tailgate. Slice it on-site to keep it from falling apart while being transported.

1. In a bowl combine dried tomatoes and enough boiling water to cover. Let stand 10 minutes; drain. Place tomatoes in a food processor; cover and process until finely chopped.

2. Meanwhile, split Italian loaf in half horizontally. Remove some soft bread from the bottom half of the loaf, leaving a ½-inch shell.

3. Spread cream cheese on cut sides of both bread halves. Spread top half with finely chopped tomatoes and bottom half with pesto. Layer provolone cheese, salami, banana pepper, and red onion on pesto. Replace top half, spread side down.

4. Slice loaf crosswise into eight sandwiches. If desired, spear a pickled pepper and/or an olive on a long pick; insert through each sandwich.

PER SERVING *441 cal., 25 g fat (10 g sat. fat), 29 mg chol., 1,234 mg sodium, 34 g carb., 3 g fiber, 18 g pro.*

START TO FINISH 25 minutes

8 servings	ingredients	16 servings
¾ cup	dried tomatoes (not oil-packed)	1½ cups
one 16-oz. loaf	Italian or French bread	two 16-oz. loaves
half 8-oz. pkg.	cream cheese, softened	one 8-oz. pkg.
⅓ cup	basil pesto	⅔ cup
4 oz.	thinly sliced provolone cheese	8 oz.
8 oz.	thinly sliced peppered salami or regular salami	1 lb.
1	fresh banana pepper, seeded and sliced	2
½	red onion, thinly sliced	1
	Small pickled chile peppers and/or pimiento-stuffed green olives (optional)	

Meatball Sliders

The meatballs and sauce simmer away in a slow cooker while you finish other party prep. When they're done, switch the cooker to the warm setting and serve right from it.

1. Place onion wedges in a 3½- or 4-qt. slow cooker. Top with frozen meatballs. In a medium bowl combine marinara sauce, balsamic vinegar, and crushed red pepper. Pour over meatballs.

2. Cover and cook on low 4 to 5 hours or high 2 to 2½ hours.

3. Stir meatballs and sauce. Place a cheese slice and a tomato slice on the bottom of each cocktail bun. Top each with a meatball; add bun tops.

PER SERVING *217 cal., 11 g fat (5 g sat. fat), 24 mg chol., 516 mg sodium, 20 g carb., 2 g fiber, 10 g pro.*

PREP 10 minutes
SLOW COOK 4 hours (low) or 2 hours (high)

12 servings	ingredients	24 servings
1	medium red onion cut into thin wedges	2
one 12-oz. pkg.	frozen cooked Italian meatballs	two 12-oz. pkg.
half 24- to 26-oz. jar	marinara or pasta sauce	one 24- to 26-oz. jar
1½ tsp.	balsamic vinegar	1 Tbsp.
¼ tsp.	crushed red pepper	½ tsp.
3	slices provolone cheese, quartered	6
2	roma tomatoes, sliced	4
12	cocktail buns, split and toasted, if desired	24

Mini Mexican Tortas

A torta is usually a generously sized Mexican sandwich. These cocktail-size sammies are perfectly scaled to be served alongside other types of party food. They start with a package (or two) of cooked pork roast au jus for fast and easy prep.

1. Transfer pork roast with juices to a medium saucepan. Using two forks, pull meat apart into shreds. Stir in pepperoncini peppers and cilantro. Cook, covered, over medium-low heat until heated through, stirring occasionally.

2. Meanwhile, for guacamole, in a medium bowl stir together onion, lime juice, garlic, and salt. Add avocados; coarsely mash avocados until mixture is combined.

3. Using a slotted spoon or a fork, divide pork mixture among bottom halves of buns. Top with guacamole and bun tops.

PER SERVING *217 cal., 12 g fat (3 g sat. fat), 37 mg chol., 443 mg sodium, 15 g carb., 5 g fiber, 16 g pro.*

START TO FINISH 25 minutes

8 servings	ingredients	16 servings
one 15-oz. pkg.	refrigerated cooked pork roast au jus	two 15-oz. pkg.
¼ cup	chopped pepperoncini peppers	½ cup
¼ cup	snipped fresh cilantro	½ cup
2 Tbsp.	finely chopped red onion	¼ cup
2 Tbsp.	fresh lime juice	¼ cup
2	cloves garlic, minced	4
¼ tsp.	salt	½ tsp.
2	avocados, halved, seeded, and peeled	4
8	tea- or cocktail-size buns (about 1½-inch diameter)	16

Louisiana Beer Chicken Wings with Chive Ranch Dressing

Marinating the wings in a spicy buttermilk bath not only infuses them with tangy flavor but it also acts as a brine, making the wings tender and juicy.

1. Place chicken wings, 3 cups of the buttermilk, and hot sauce in a large resealable plastic bag set in a shallow dish. Seal bag; turn to coat chicken. Marinate 2 to 8 hours. Drain wings and pat dry; discard bag and marinade then place wings in new large resealable plastic bag.

2. For the rub, in a small bowl stir together cayenne pepper, 1 Tbsp. black pepper, oregano, and 1 tsp. of the garlic powder. Sprinkle rub over chicken wings; seal bag. Shake bag to coat wings. If desired, refrigerate 6 to 24 hours.

3. Preheat oven to 200°F. Prepare grill for indirect heat. Place half the wings on grill rack over drip pan. Grill, covered, 20 to 25 minutes or until chicken is no longer pink, turning once. Transfer wings to a shallow baking pan. Keep warm in oven while grilling remaining wings.

4. Meanwhile, for Louisiana Beer Sauce, in a saucepan cook onion and sweet pepper in hot oil over medium heat 4 minutes or until tender. In a bowl stir together beer, water, cornstarch, Cajun seasoning, and half the salt. Add beer mixture to onion mixture. Cook and stir until sauce is thickened and bubbly. Cook and stir 2 minutes more.

5. For Chive Ranch Dressing, in a bowl whisk together sour cream, remaining buttermilk, chives, lemon juice, and remaining garlic powder, salt, and black pepper. Cover and refrigerate until serving.

6. Place wings in an extra-large bowl; drizzle with sauce and toss to coat. Transfer wings to a serving bowl or platter with dressing. If desired, serve with carrot and celery sticks.

FOR 24 SERVINGS In Step 1, use 6 cups of the buttermilk and two plastic bags. In Step 2, use 2 Tbsp. black pepper and 2 tsp. garlic powder.

PER SERVING *108 cal., 7 g fat (2 g sat. fat), 50 mg chol., 126 mg sodium, 2 g carb., 0 g fiber, 8 g pro.*

PREP 20 minutes
MARINATE 2 hours   **GRILL** 20 minutes

12 servings	ingredients	24 servings
24	whole chicken wings	48
3⅓ cups	buttermilk	6⅔ cups
2 Tbsp.	bottled hot sauce	¼ cup
1 Tbsp.	cayenne pepper	2 Tbsp.
1 Tbsp.	black pepper	2 Tbsp.
1 Tbsp.	dried oregano, crushed	2 Tbsp.
1½ tsp.	garlic powder	1 Tbsp.
¼ cup	chopped onion	½ cup
¼ cup	chopped red sweet pepper	½ cup
1 Tbsp.	vegetable oil	2 Tbsp.
½ cup	beer	1 cup
½ cup	cold water	1 cup
1 Tbsp.	cornstarch	2 Tbsp.
1 Tbsp.	Cajun seasoning	2 Tbsp.
½ tsp.	salt	1 tsp.
½ cup	sour cream	1 cup
2 Tbsp.	snipped fresh chives	¼ cup
2 tsp.	fresh lemon juice	4 tsp.
⅛ tsp.	black pepper	¼ tsp.
	Carrot and celery sticks (optional)	

Watermelon-Berry Lemonade

This super-summery and refreshing lemonade is a smart choice for a party that involves all ages. Serve as is or invite adult guests to spike it with a little vodka, gin, or rum, if desired.

1. In a blender combine half the watermelon, strawberries, and lemonade concentrate. Cover; blend until smooth. Transfer to serving containers. Repeat with remaining watermelon, strawberries, and lemonade concentrate. Add water; chill up to 2 days.

2. Serve over ice with watermelon wedges, fresh strawberries, and/or lemon slices, if desired.

FOR 24 SERVINGS In Step 1, make lemonade in four batches.

MAKE AHEAD Cover and refrigerate up to 2 days. To serve, stir and add berries and watermelon wedges.

PER SERVING *145 cal., 0 g fat, 0 mg chol., 8 mg sodium, 37 g carb., 1 g fiber, 1 g pro.*

PREP 25 minutes
CHILL 24 hours

12 servings	ingredients	24 servings
8 cups	cubed seeded watermelon	16 cups
3 cups	hulled and quartered strawberries	6 cups
two 12-oz. cans	frozen lemonade concentrate, thawed	four 12-oz. cans
8 cups	water	16 cups
	fresh watermelon wedges (optional)	
	Whole hulled fresh strawberries (optional)	
	Fresh lemon slices (optional)	

Strawberry Agua Fresca

"Agua fresca" means "cool waters" or literally "fresh waters" in Spanish. This concoction of water, fruits, lime juice, and sweeteners offers a tasty way to cool down on a hot day.

1. In a blender combine half the halved strawberries and half the cold water. Cover and blend well. Strain mixture through a fine-mesh sieve into a pitcher or large glass jar. Discard solids. Repeat, using remaining strawberries and water.

2. Stir in lime juice and ¼ cup honey. Chill until ready to serve.

3. Serve in ice-filled glasses. Garnish with whole strawberries and lime slices. If desired, sweeten to taste with additional honey.

FOR 12 SERVINGS In Step 1, make strawberry mixture in four batches. In Step 2, use ½ cup honey.

PER SERVING *93 cal., 0 g fat, 0 mg chol., 6 mg sodium, 24 g carb., 2 g fiber, 1 g pro.*

START TO FINISH 20 minutes

6 servings	ingredients	12 servings
6 cups	fresh strawberries, hulled and halved	12 cups
4 cups	cold water	8 cups
¼ cup	freshly squeezed lime juice	½ cup
¼ cup	honey	½ cup
	Ice cubes	
	Whole fresh strawberries	
	Fresh lime slices	
	Honey (optional)	

Ginger Beer Shandy

If you are a fan of spicy ginger flavor, substitute ginger beer (a peppery-tasting nonalcoholic soda) for the ginger ale.

1. If desired, wet rims of eight 16-oz. beer glasses or mugs with lemon slice. Dip rims into a dish of finely chopped crystallized ginger to coat.

2. In a large pitcher combine chopped crystallized ginger and lemon juice. Using a muddler or the back of a spoon, crush ginger against side of pitcher. Slowly pour beer and ginger ale down side of pitcher; stir gently. Serve in prepared or chilled glasses or mugs and top with lemon slices.

PER SERVING *151 cal., 0 g fat, 0 mg chol., 20 mg sodium, 24 g carb., 1 g fiber, 1 g pro.*

START TO FINISH 15 minutes

8 servings	ingredients	16 servings
	Lemon slice and finely chopped crystallized ginger (optional)	
3 Tbsp.	chopped crystallized ginger	¼ cup + 2 Tbsp.
3 Tbsp.	lemon juice	¼ cup + 2 Tbsp.
five 12-oz. cans	chilled lager or pilsner beer	ten 12-oz. cans
4 cups	ginger ale, chilled	8 cups

CHAPTER 2

Poultry

Poultry is popular for two good reasons. It's inexpensive and its mild flavor lends itself to dressing up in all kinds of delicious ways.

39

53

57

Grilled Chicken with Lemon-Cucumber Relish

This Greek-style grilled chicken makes a welcome and tasty meal on a warm summer night when you want to get something fresh on the table fast.

1. Remove ½ tsp. zest and 2 Tbsp. juice from lemon; set aside. Brush chicken breast halves with olive oil; sprinkle with the next three ingredients (through pepper). Grill chicken, covered, over medium heat 12 to 15 minutes or until done (165°F), turning once.

2. Meanwhile, for relish, in a bowl combine lemon zest and juice and the next four ingredients (through garlic); stir to combine. For yogurt sauce, in a bowl stir together remaining ingredients. Top chicken with relish and drizzle with yogurt sauce.

FOR 8 SERVINGS In Step 1, remove 1 tsp. zest and ¼ cup juice from lemons.

PER SERVING *310 cal., 17 g fat (4 g sat. fat), 82 mg chol., 369 mg sodium, 12 g carb., 1 g fiber, 28 g pro.*

PREP 20 minutes
GRILL 12 minutes

4 servings	ingredients	8 servings
1	lemon	2
4 (1½ to 2 lb.)	skinless, boneless chicken breast halves	8 (3 to 4 lb.)
1 to 2 Tbsp.	olive oil	2 to 4 Tbsp.
2 tsp.	ground cumin	4 tsp.
½ tsp.	salt	1 tsp.
¼ tsp.	cracked black pepper	½ tsp.
2½ cups	chopped seedless cucumber	5 cups
1 cup	chopped tomato	2 cups
¼ cup	finely chopped onion	½ cup
2	cloves garlic, minced	4
⅓ cup	plain Greek yogurt	⅔ cup
1 Tbsp.	honey	2 Tbsp.
1 Tbsp.	milk	2 Tbsp.

Orange-Ginger Chicken Stir-Fry

Serving this Asian-style stir-fry over quinoa instead of rice cuts the carb count and increases the protein. Quinoa has the highest protein content of any grain.

1. In a wok or large skillet heat 1 Tbsp. of the oil over medium heat. Add carrots; cook and stir 5 minutes. Add sweet pepper; cook and stir 3 minutes more or until carrots are tender. Transfer to a medium bowl. Add another 1 Tbsp. oil to wok; heat over medium-high heat. Add chicken; cook and stir 4 to 5 minutes or until no longer pink. Add to carrot mixture; stir in edamame.

2. Add remaining oil to wok; heat over medium heat. Add next three ingredients (through crushed red pepper); cook and stir 30 seconds. Stir in next three ingredients (through soy sauce). Bring to boiling.

3. Combine cornstarch and cold water; stir into broth mixture. Simmer 2 minutes. Return chicken mixture to wok; heat through. Serve over quinoa; sprinkle with sesame seeds and, if desired, additional crushed red pepper.

FOR 12 SERVINGS In Step 1, use 2 Tbsp. oil to cook carrots and sweet peppers, and an additional 2 Tbsp. to cook chicken.

PER SERVING *373 cal., 13 g fat (2 g sat. fat), 48 mg chol., 481 mg sodium, 39 g carb., 7 g fiber, 26 g pro.*

START TO FINISH 45 minutes

6 servings	ingredients	12 servings
3 Tbsp.	olive oil	¼ cup + 2 Tbsp.
1 lb.	carrots, cut into thin bite-size strips	2 lb.
1	red sweet pepper, cut into thin bite-size strips	2
1 lb.	skinless, boneless chicken breast halves, cut into 1-inch pieces	2 lb.
1 cup	frozen edamame, thawed	2 cups
1 Tbsp.	grated fresh ginger	2 Tbsp.
3	cloves garlic, minced	6
½ tsp.	crushed red pepper (optional)	1 tsp.
1½ cups	reduced-sodium chicken broth	3 cups
¼ cup	frozen orange juice concentrate, thawed	½ cup
2 Tbsp.	reduced-sodium soy sauce	¼ cup
2 Tbsp.	cornstarch	¼ cup
2 Tbsp.	cold water	¼ cup
3 cups	hot cooked quinoa	6 cups
1 Tbsp.	sesame seeds, toasted (tip, page 8)	2 Tbsp.

Mojo Chicken Fajitas with Orange-Avocado Salsa

Mojo is a Cuban marinade and sauce spiked with the fresh flavors of citrus, garlic, and olive oil. As with any marinated dish, the longer you let it soak the more flavor it has. The chicken can sit in the marinade up to 24 hours. Make the salsa 4 hours ahead and the fajitas come together fast when you're ready to cook.

1. Place chicken in a resealable plastic bag set in a shallow dish. For marinade, in a small bowl combine next seven ingredients (through cumin). Pour marinade over chicken. Seal bag; turn to coat. Marinate in the refrigerator 2 to 24 hours, turning bag occasionally. Meanwhile, prepare Orange-Avocado Salsa; cover and chill.

2. Drain chicken, reserving marinade. Brush sweet peppers and onions with some of the marinade; discard remaining marinade.

3. Grill chicken, uncovered, over medium heat 12 to 15 minutes or until a thermometer registers 165°F. Grill onions the last 10 to 12 minutes and peppers the last 8 to 10 minutes or until vegetables are crisp-tender, turning occasionally.

4. Meanwhile, if desired, peel off and discard skins from peppers. Cut peppers into thin strips and chop onions. Slice chicken. Serve chicken and vegetables on tortillas with Orange-Avocado Salsa and sour cream. If desired, sprinkle with cilantro and serve with lime wedges.

ORANGE-AVOCADO SALSA In a medium bowl combine 2 medium oranges, peeled, sectioned, and chopped; 1 large ripe avocado, halved, seeded, peeled, and chopped; ¼ cup each chopped red onion and snipped fresh cilantro; 2 Tbsp. lime juice; ½ to 1 tsp. bottled hot pepper sauce; and ¼ tsp. salt. If desired, cover and chill up to 4 hours.

***TIP** To warm tortillas, wrap them tightly in foil and place on grill the last 10 minutes of grilling, turning once.

PER SERVING *724 cal., 29 g fat (0 g sat. fat), 72 mg chol., 744 mg sodium, 79 g carb., 8 g fiber, 39 g pro.*

PREP 45 minutes
MARINATE 2 hours   **GRILL** 12 minutes

6 servings	ingredients	12 servings
1 lb.	boneless, skinless chicken breast halves	2 lb.
⅓ cup	olive oil	⅔ cup
⅓ cup	orange juice	⅔ cup
⅓ cup	lime juice	⅔ cup
¼ cup	chopped onion	½ cup
6	cloves garlic, minced	12
1 tsp.	dried oregano, crushed	2 tsp.
1 tsp.	ground cumin	2 tsp.
1 recipe	Orange-Avocado Salsa	2 recipes
2	red sweet peppers, quartered lengthwise	4
2	medium onions, cut into thick slices	4
12	6-inch flour tortillas, warmed*	24
¼ cup	sour cream	½ cup
	Fresh cilantro leaves and/or lime wedges (optional)	

Chicken Noodle Bowls with Coconut Peanut Sauce

If you like your curry spicy, use hot curry powder in this dish—or try half hot curry powder and half regular curry powder.

PREP 35 minutes
MARINATE 4 hours **COOK** 15 minutes

4 servings	ingredients	8 servings
two 8-oz.	skinless, boneless chicken breast halves	four 8-oz.
one 14.5-oz. can	light or regular coconut milk*	two 14.5-oz. cans
¼ cup	lime juice	½ cup
1 tsp.	curry powder	2 tsp.
½ tsp.	salt	1 tsp.
	Nonstick cooking spray	
1 Tbsp.	creamy peanut butter	2 Tbsp.
1 Tbsp.	honey	2 Tbsp.
⅛ to ¼ tsp.	cayenne pepper	¼ to ½ tsp.
4 oz.	Pad Thai-style dry rice noodles, cooked according to package directions, cooled	8 oz.
2 tsp.	sesame oil or canola oil	4 tsp.
2 cups	fresh baby spinach leaves	4 cups
1	red sweet pepper, cut into thin bite-size strips	2
½ cup	sliced green onion tops	1 cup
1	lime, cut into wedges	2
	Fresh cilantro leaves	
¼ cup	coarsely chopped unsalted roasted peanuts (optional)	½ cup

1. Slice chicken in half horizontally. Place chicken in a resealable plastic bag set in a medium bowl. In a small bowl combine ¾ cup of coconut milk, the lime juice, and curry powder. Pour over chicken in bag. Seal bag; turn to coat. Marinate in the refrigerator 4 to 12 hours.

2. Drain chicken; discard marinade. Sprinkle chicken with half the salt. Coat a large nonstick skillet with cooking spray; heat over medium-high heat. Add chicken; cook 8 to 9 minutes or until done (165°F), turning once.

3. When chicken is done, transfer chicken to a cutting board; keep warm. Add ¾ cup water, peanut butter, honey, and cayenne pepper to the skillet; cook over medium-low heat, whisking constantly, until smooth. Whisk in remaining coconut milk. Heat through.

4. In a large bowl toss together cold noodles, oil, and remaining salt. Add spinach, sweet pepper, and green onion tops.

5. Thinly slice chicken crosswise. Divide noodles and vegetables among four serving bowls. Top with chicken. Pour hot Coconut Peanut Milk sauce over each serving. Serve with lime wedges, cilantro, and, if desired, peanuts.

*TIP Coconut milk separates in the can; pour into a bowl and whisk until combined before measuring.

FOR 8 SERVINGS In Step 1, use 1½ cups coconut milk. In Step 2, cook half the chicken at a time. In Step 3, use 1½ cups water.

PER SERVING *351 cal., 11 g fat, 82 mg chol., 427 mg sodium, 33 g carb., 2 g fiber, 30 g pro.*

Tandoori-Spiced Chicken and Rice Bake

Two Indian-inspired favorites come together in this one-dish dinner. Aromatic tandoori-style chicken is baked in a tomatoey coconut milk sauce reminiscent of many popular curry dishes.

1. Preheat oven to 350°F. Lightly coat a 2-qt. shallow baking dish with cooking spray; set aside.

2. Sprinkle 1½ tsp. Tandoori Spice Blend over chicken; rub in with your fingers. In a large skillet heat half the oil over medium-high heat. Add chicken; cook 8 minutes or until chicken is done (165°F), turning once. Remove from skillet.

3. In the same skillet heat the remaining oil over medium heat. Add onion, carrot, sweet pepper, and Anaheim pepper; cook 2 minutes, stirring occasionally. Add zucchini and garlic; cook and stir 2 minutes more.

4. Stir in broth, coconut milk, rice, water, tomato paste, and remaining Tandoori Spice Blend. Bring to boiling; reduce heat. Simmer 15 to 20 minutes. Slice chicken; stir into vegetable mixture.

5. Transfer chicken mixture to the prepared baking dish. Bake, covered, 20 minutes or until heated through and rice is tender. Sprinkle with cilantro before serving.

TANDOORI SPICE BLEND In a bowl stir together 1 tsp. yellow curry powder, 1 tsp. garam masala, ½ tsp. ground ginger, ½ tsp. ground cumin, ½ tsp. ground coriander, ½ tsp. ground cardamom, ¼ tsp. salt, ⅛ tsp. ground cinnamon, and ⅛ tsp. black pepper.

FOR 8 SERVINGS In Step 1, use a 3- to 4-qt. shallow baking dish. In Step 2, use 1 Tbsp. of Tandoori Spice Blend.

PER SERVING *438 cal., 15 g fat (5 g sat. fat), 91 mg chol., 586 mg sodium, 38 g carb., 3 g fiber, 37 g pro.*

PREP 45 minutes
BAKE 20 minutes

4 servings	ingredients	8 servings
	Nonstick cooking spray	
1 recipe	Tandoori Spice Blend or purchased tandoori blend	2 recipes
four 4-oz.	skinless, boneless chicken breast halves	eight 4-oz.
2 Tbsp.	vegetable oil	¼ cup
½ cup	coarsely chopped onion	1 cup
½ cup	coarsely shredded carrot	1 cup
½ cup	chopped red sweet pepper	1 cup
½	Anaheim pepper, seeded and chopped (tip, page 15)	1
1	zucchini, halved lengthwise, sliced ¼ inch thick	2
2	cloves garlic, thinly sliced	4
one 14.5-oz. can	reduced-sodium chicken broth	two 14.5-oz. cans
1 cup	light or regular coconut milk (tip, page 34)	2 cups
⅔ cup	uncooked long grain rice	1⅓ cups
½ cup	water	1 cup
¼ cup	no-salt-added tomato paste	½ cup
	Snipped fresh cilantro	

Chicken with Breadsticks Bake

PREP 25 minutes
BAKE 18 minutes

4 servings	ingredients	8 servings
2 cups	frozen mixed vegetables	4 cups
one 11-oz. pkg.	refrigerated breadsticks	two 11-oz. pkg.
½ cup	all-purpose flour	1 cup
½ tsp.	ground sage	1 tsp.
¼ tsp.	salt	½ tsp.
¼ tsp.	black pepper	½ tsp.
12 oz.	skinless, boneless chicken breast halves, cut into bite-size pieces	24 oz.
2 Tbsp.	vegetable oil	¼ cup
one 14.5-oz. can	reduced-sodium chicken broth	two 14.5-oz. cans
½ cup	milk	1 cup
½ cup	shredded Mexican cheese blend	1 cup
	Chopped chives (optional)	

When you're craving the comfort of chicken pot pie but don't have the time to make that labor-intensive dish, these individual chicken gratins will hit the spot.

1. Preheat oven to 400°F. Place vegetables in a sieve or colander. Run cold water over vegetables to thaw. Separate breadsticks; set aside.

2. In a resealable plastic bag combine flour, sage, salt, and pepper. Add chicken pieces in batches, shaking to coat. In a large skillet heat oil over medium-high heat. Add chicken; sprinkle with any remaining flour mixture. Cook and stir 2 minutes or until browned. Add broth, milk, and vegetables. Bring to boiling, stirring once.

3. Divide chicken mixture among four 16-oz. gratin dishes or individual casseroles. Arrange three breadsticks across the top of each dish. Sprinkle with cheese. Bake 18 minutes or until breadsticks are browned and filling is bubbly. If desired, sprinkle with chopped chives.

FOR 8 SERVINGS In Step 3, use eight 16-oz. gratin dishes or individual casseroles.

PER SERVING *544 cal., 17 g fat (7 g sat. fat), 64 mg chol., 1,138 mg sodium, 61 g carb., 4 g fiber, 35 g pro.*

Chicken Saltimbocca

A simple slaw of crunchy fennel and red onion adds a fresh touch to this classic Italian dish. Pancetta is cured but unsmoked Italian bacon. It comes in very thin round slices.

PREP 35 minutes
BAKE 12 minutes

4 servings	ingredients	8 servings
2 Tbsp.	olive oil	¼ cup
8	thin slices pancetta	16
four 6-oz.	skinless, boneless chicken breast halves, pounded to ½-inch thickness	eight 6-oz.
½ tsp.	salt	1 tsp.
½ tsp.	black pepper	1 tsp.
2 Tbsp.	fresh marjoram or oregano leaves	¼ cup
1 bulb	fennel, trimmed, halved, cored, and thinly sliced	2 bulbs
1	small red onion, thinly sliced	2

1. Preheat oven to 375°F. In an extra-large skillet heat half the oil over medium heat. Add pancetta; cook 30 to 60 seconds or until it starts to brown. Remove from skillet. Increase heat to medium-high.

2. Season chicken with half the salt and pepper. Add chicken to skillet; cook 4 to 5 minutes until golden. Turn; cook 1 minute more. Transfer to a shallow baking pan. Top with half the marjoram and the pancetta.

3. Bake 12 to 15 minutes or until chicken is done (165°F). Meanwhile, in a medium bowl toss together fennel and onion. Drizzle with remaining oil; season with remaining salt and pepper. Serve with chicken. Sprinkle with remaining marjoram.

PER SERVING *377 cal., 20 g fat (5 g sat. fat), 136 mg chol., 575 mg sodium, 6 g carb., 2 g fiber, 42 g pro.*

Chicken and Chickpea Buddha Bowls

Crunchy roasted chickpeas have become a popular snack food. Look for them—spiced in a variety of flavors—in the health foods section of your supermarket.

1. Preheat oven to 425°F. In an extra-large baking pan combine squash and shallots. Drizzle with oil and sprinkle with half the salt and the pepper. Toss to coat; spread in a single layer. Roast 20 to 25 minutes or until squash is tender, stirring twice.

2. Meanwhile, in a medium saucepan cook green beans, covered, in a small amount of boiling water 6 to 8 minutes or just until beans are tender; drain. Rinse with cold water; drain well.

3. In a bowl combine lemon juice, garlic, and remaining salt. Add kale. Toss and rub kale leaves gently with your fingers until kale is well coated and leaves start to look wilted and glossy.

4. Divide kale, squash, green beans, and chicken among serving bowls. Drizzle with Sesame-Dijon Dressing and top with chickpeas.

SESAME-DIJON DRESSING In a bowl whisk together ½ cup tahini (sesame seed paste), ½ cup water, 3 Tbsp. each lemon juice and honey, 2 Tbsp. olive oil, 1 Tbsp. Dijon mustard, and ¼ tsp. salt. Makes 1½ cups. Transfer unused dressing to an airtight container; cover and chill up to 3 days.

PER SERVING *321 cal., 14 g fat (2 g sat. fat), 30 mg chol., 530 mg sodium, 34 g carb., 6 g fiber, 20 g pro.*

PREP 35 minutes
ROAST 20 minutes

4 servings	ingredients	8 servings
2 cups	¾-inch cubes peeled butternut squash	4 cups
2	shallots, cut into thin wedges	4
2 tsp.	olive oil	4 tsp.
½ tsp.	salt	1 tsp.
⅛ tsp.	black pepper	¼ tsp.
1½ cups	halved fresh green beans, trimmed if desired	3 cups
1 Tbsp.	lemon juice	2 Tbsp.
2	cloves garlic, minced	4
4 cups	torn fresh kale	8 cups
1 cup	chopped cooked chicken breast	2 cups
½ cup	Sesame-Dijon Dressing	1 cup
½ cup	crunchy Bombay spice or falafel-flavor chickpeas	1 cup

Chicken Tender Kabobs

To ensure that the chicken and vegetables all cook evenly, leave a little bit of space between each piece of food when threading the skewers—don't pack them too tightly.

PREP 20 minutes
GRILL 10 minutes

4 servings	ingredients	8 servings
⅓ cup	plain Greek yogurt	⅔ cup
¼ cup	light mayonnaise	½ cup
2 Tbsp.	water	¼ cup
1 tsp.	sriracha	2 tsp.
½ tsp.	salt	1 tsp.
one 8-oz. pkg.	cremini or button mushrooms, stemmed	two 8-oz. pkg.
2 Tbsp.	olive oil	¼ cup
2 Tbsp.	red wine vinegar	¼ cup
1 tsp.	dried oregano, crushed	2 tsp.
1 tsp.	ground cumin	2 tsp.
¼ tsp.	black pepper	½ tsp.
8	chicken breast tenderloins	16
8	miniature sweet peppers	16

1. For yogurt sauce, in a bowl combine yogurt, mayonnaise, water, sriracha sauce, and half the salt. Cover and chill until ready to serve.

2. In a large saucepan cook mushrooms in boiling water 1 minute; drain and pat dry. In a large bowl whisk together oil, vinegar, oregano, cumin, black pepper, and remaining salt. Add mushrooms, chicken, and sweet peppers; toss to coat.

3. On four 12-inch skewers* alternately thread chicken (accordian-style), mushrooms, and sweet peppers. Grease grill rack. Grill chicken kabobs, covered, over medium heat 10 to 12 minutes or until done (165°F), turning once.

4. Serve kabobs with yogurt sauce and, if desired, additional sriracha.

*TIP If using wooden skewers, soak in water 30 minutes.

FOR 8 SERVINGS In Step 3, use eight 12-inch skewers.

PER SERVING *262 cal., 15 g fat (3 g sat. fat), 69 mg chol., 472 mg sodium, 9 g carb., 2 g fiber, 24 g pro.*

Korean-Style Chili-Garlic Chicken Stir-Fry

A sweet-spicy melange of pickled cabbage, carrots, and red onion gives this light and healthful stir-fry a pleasantly tangy finishing touch.

1. Prepare Quick-Pickled Vegetables.

2. In a medium bowl combine next five ingredients (through garlic). Transfer half the mixture to a small bowl. Add chicken to the remaining mixture in medium bowl. Toss to coat. Add honey and cornstarch to soy sauce mixture in separate bowl, stirring to dissolve cornstarch.

3. In a large wok or nonstick skillet cook beans in just enough boiling water to cover 4 minutes or just until crisp-tender; drain beans in colander. Wipe wok dry.

4. In the same wok heat oils over medium-high heat. Add onion and sweet pepper; cook and stir 4 to 5 minutes or until crisp-tender. Remove vegetables from wok. Add half the chicken to wok; cook and stir over medium-high heat 3 to 4 minutes or until chicken is no longer pink. Remove chicken from wok. Repeat with remaining chicken. Return chicken, green beans, onion, and red pepper to wok. Stir sauce; add to wok. Cook and stir until thickened.

5. Spoon drained Quick-Pickled Vegetables over stir-fry. Top with sesame seeds.

QUICK-PICKLED VEGETABLES In a saucepan combine ½ cup each water and rice vinegar, ¼ cup sugar, ½ tsp. salt, and ⅛ tsp. crushed red pepper. Bring to boiling; reduce heat. Simmer, uncovered, 2 minutes. Remove from heat. Add 1 cup coarsely shredded napa cabbage, ½ cup each shredded carrots and thinly sliced quartered red onion, and 1 tsp. finely chopped fresh ginger; stir until well combined. Cover; let stand at room temperature 30 to 60 minutes. Drain before serving.

PER SERVING *344 cal., 11 g fat (2 g sat. fat), 83 mg chol., 564 mg sodium, 32 g carb., 4 g fiber, 29 g pro.*

PREP 25 minutes
COOK 15 minutes

4 servings	ingredients	8 servings
1 recipe	Quick-Pickled Vegetables	2 recipes
2 Tbsp.	reduced-sodium soy sauce	¼ cup
2 Tbsp.	rice vinegar	¼ cup
1 Tbsp.	Asian chili-garlic sauce	2 Tbsp.
1 Tbsp.	finely chopped fresh ginger	2 Tbsp.
3	cloves garlic, minced	6
1 lb.	skinless, boneless chicken breast halves, cut into 1-inch pieces	2 lb.
3 Tbsp.	honey or packed brown sugar	¼ cup + 2 Tbsp.
2 tsp.	cornstarch	4 tsp.
8 oz.	fresh green beans, trimmed	1 lb.
1 Tbsp.	toasted sesame oil	2 Tbsp.
1 Tbsp.	canola oil	2 Tbsp.
½ cup	coarsely chopped onion	1 cup
¾ cup	coarsely chopped red sweet pepper	1½ cups
2 tsp.	sesame seeds, toasted (tip, page 8)	4 tsp.

Spicy Buffalo Chicken Salad

4 servings	ingredients	8 servings
1 lb.	skinless, boneless chicken breast halves	2 lb.
2 Tbsp.	olive oil	¼ cup
1 Tbsp.	cider vinegar	2 Tbsp.
1 Tbsp.	bottled hot pepper sauce	2 Tbsp.
⅓ cup	bottled blue cheese salad dressing	⅔ cup
½ tsp.	bottled hot pepper sauce	1 tsp.
2 cups	shredded savoy or green cabbage	4 cups
1 cup	bite-size carrot strips	2 cups
1 cup	thinly sliced celery	2 cups
½ cup	crumbled blue cheese	1 cup

Savoy cabbage has pretty, crinkly leaves that have a more tender texture than regular green cabbage. It's a great choice for eating raw in salads, but if you can't find it, green cabbage works well.

1. Place chicken in a large resealable plastic bag set in a shallow dish. For marinade, in a small bowl stir together oil, vinegar, and the 1 Tbsp. hot pepper sauce. Pour over chicken in bag; seal bag. Turn to coat chicken. Marinate in the refrigerator 3 to 4 hours, turning bag occasionally.

2. Drain chicken, reserving marinade. Grill chicken, uncovered, directly over medium heat 12 to 15 minutes or until chicken is done (165°F), turning and brushing once with reserved marinade. Discard any remaining marinade. Slice chicken diagonally.

3. In a serving bowl stir together salad dressing and ½ tsp. hot pepper sauce. Add cabbage, carrot strips, celery, and three-fourths of the blue cheese. Toss to coat. Arrange sliced chicken on top of salad. Sprinkle with remaining blue cheese.

FOR 8 SERVINGS In Step 1, use 2 Tbsp. hot pepper sauce. In Step 3, use 1 tsp. hot pepper sauce.

PER SERVING *367 cal., 23 g fat (6 g sat. fat), 80 mg chol., 563 mg sodium, 8 g carb., 3 g fiber, 32 g pro.*

Chicken Sandwiches with Roasted Pepper and Goat Cheese Spread

These grilled chicken sandwiches are perfect to make when you want to have friends over for a casual backyard barbecue but would like a change-up from burgers. Serve with a side of crunchy sweet potato chips, if you like.

PREP 30 minutes
MARINATE 1 hour   **GRILL** 9 minutes

4 servings	ingredients	8 servings
4	skinless, boneless chicken breast halves	8
¼ cup	balsamic vinegar	½ cup
2 Tbsp.	olive oil	¼ cup
1 Tbsp.	snipped fresh rosemary	2 Tbsp.
2	cloves garlic, minced	4
	Salt and black pepper	
one 10- to 12-inch	rosemary or garlic focaccia	two 10- to 12-inch
1 recipe	Roasted Pepper and Goat Cheese Spread	2 recipes
1 cup	fresh baby spinach or small romaine lettuce leaves	2 cups
½	red onion, thinly sliced	1

1. Place each chicken piece between plastic wrap and pound with flat side of a meat mallet to ½-inch thickness. Place chicken in a resealable plastic bag set in a shallow dish. For marinade, in a small bowl combine next four ingredients (through garlic); pour over chicken. Seal bag; turn to coat chicken. Marinate in the refrigerator 1 to 2 hours, turning bag occasionally.

2. Drain chicken, discarding marinade. Lightly sprinkle chicken with salt and pepper. Grill chicken over medium heat 9 to 11 minutes or until done (165°F), turning once.

3. Meanwhile, cut bread into four wedges; cut wedges in half horizontally. Add bread, cut sides down, to grill the last 2 minutes of grilling.

4. Spread toasted sides of bread with Roasted Pepper and Goat Cheese Spread. Layer chicken, spinach, and red onion between wedges.

ROASTED PEPPER AND GOAT CHEESE SPREAD In a food processor combine 4 oz. soft goat cheese (chèvre), ¼ cup roasted red sweet pepper, 1 tsp. liquid from roasted peppers, and 1 tsp. snipped fresh rosemary. Cover and process until nearly smooth. (Or finely chop the roasted pepper and stir together with a spoon.)

PER SERVING *321 cal., 12 g fat (5 g sat. fat), 96 mg chol., 392 mg sodium, 11 g carb., 1 g fiber, 40 g pro.*

Beer-Braised Chicken Tacos

Braising chicken thighs in a jalapeño-spiked liquid of Mexican beer and chicken broth ensures the cooked meat will be juicy and flavorful.

1. In a large saucepan bring beer, broth, and jalapeño to boiling. Add chicken; reduce heat. Simmer, covered, 20 to 25 minutes or until chicken is done (170°F), turning once. Remove chicken. When cool enough to handle, discard skin and bones. Shred chicken using two forks. Skim fat from cooking liquid and remove jalapeño. Set aside.

2. In a large skillet heat oil over medium heat. Add onion; cook 5 minutes or until tender, stirring occasionally. Stir in cumin and coriander. Add salsa and ½ cup of the cooking liquid. Bring to boiling. Stir in chicken; reduce heat. Cook 7 minutes or until mixture is thickened, stirring occasionally. (For spicier filling, chop the reserved jalapeño and add to chicken mixture.)

3. Fill warm tortillas with shredded chicken and serve with slaw, radishes, and/or sour cream.

FOR 8 SERVINGS In Step 2, add 1 cup of the cooking liquid.

PER SERVING *470 cal., 21 g fat (5 g sat. fat), 153 mg chol., 550 mg sodium, 22 g carb., 4 g fiber, 46 g pro.*

PREP 20 minutes
COOK 35 minutes

4 servings	ingredients	8 servings
one 12-oz. bottle	Mexican beer	two 12-oz. bottles
1 cup	chicken broth or water	2 cups
1	jalapeño, quartered lengthwise and seeded (tip, page 15)	2
1½ lb.	bone-in chicken thighs	3 lb.
2 tsp.	vegetable oil	4 tsp.
⅓ cup	chopped onion	⅔ cup
1 tsp.	ground cumin	2 tsp.
1 tsp.	ground coriander	2 tsp.
1 cup	salsa verde	2 cups
8	6-inch corn or flour tortillas, warmed	16
	Cabbage slaw, pickled radishes, and/or sour cream	

Quick Tandoori-Style Chicken

Basmati rice has a nutty flavor and fragrance. It is almost exclusively the type of rice served with all kinds of Indian foods and definitely worth keeping on hand to add a touch of authenticity to Indian-style dishes.

PREP 15 minutes
MARINATE 15 minutes   **GRILL** 8 minutes

4 servings	ingredients	8 servings
½ cup	plain Greek yogurt	1 cup
1 Tbsp.	cider vinegar	2 Tbsp.
2 tsp.	Madras (hot) curry powder	4 tsp.
1	clove garlic, minced	2
¼ tsp.	kosher salt	½ tsp.
1½ lb.	skinless, boneless chicken thighs, cut into 1-inch pieces	3 lb.
2 to 3 cups	hot cooked basmati rice	4 to 6 cups
	Mango chutney	
	Chopped fresh mint	

1. In a large bowl combine first five ingredients (through salt). Add chicken; toss to coat. Marinate at room temperature 15 minutes (or cover and marinate in refrigerator 2 to 24 hours, stirring occasionally).

2. Thread chicken onto skewers,* leaving ¼ inch between pieces. Grease grill rack. Grill kabobs, covered, over medium-high heat 8 to 10 minutes or until chicken is no longer pink, turning once.

3. Serve chicken over rice with mango chutney. Sprinkle with mint.

*TIP If using wooden skewers, soak in water 30 minutes.

PER SERVING *232 cal., 8 g fat (2 g sat. fat), 162 mg chol., 295 mg sodium, 2 g carb., 1 g fiber, 37 g pro.*

Spice-Rubbed Chicken and Poblano Tacos

Poblano peppers are dark green and glossy—the type of pepper traditionally stuffed with cheese and batter-fried for chiles rellenos. They have a rich, fruity flavor and sometimes a hint of heat.

1. Preheat broiler. Halve peppers lengthwise, removing seeds and stems. Arrange peppers, skin sides up, and garlic in a shallow foil-lined baking pan. Drizzle with half the oil. Broil 4 inches from heat 8 to 10 minutes or until blackened. Wrap in foil.

2. Meanwhile, stir together remaining oil, the chili powder, cumin, and half the salt. Rub over chicken. Arrange in baking pan. Broil 4 inches from heat 10 to 12 minutes or until done (170°F), turning once. Remove and slice; cover to keep warm. Add cream to hot pan.

3. Peel and slice peppers. Remove skin from garlic cloves; slice. Add peppers, garlic, and remaining salt to pan with cream. Broil 4 inches from heat 1 minute or until thickened and bubbly. Serve pepper mixture and chicken in tortillas.

PER SERVING *344 cal., 15 g fat (5 g sat. fat), 79 mg chol., 319 mg sodium, 29 g carb., 4 g fiber, 24 g pro.*

PREP 20 minutes
BROIL 18 minutes

4 servings	ingredients	8 servings
¾ lb.	poblano peppers (tip, page 15)	1½ lb.
2	cloves garlic, unpeeled	4
2 Tbsp.	vegetable oil	¼ cup
1½ tsp.	chili powder	1 Tbsp.
1 tsp.	cumin seeds, toasted and crushed (tip, page 8)	2 tsp.
½ tsp.	salt	1 tsp.
¾ lb.	skinless, boneless chicken thighs	1½ lb.
¼ cup	heavy cream	½ cup
8	6-inch corn tortillas, warmed	16

Firecracker Fried Chicken

Cool the fire of this zippy Nashville-style fried chicken with a side of warm cornbread slathered in butter and tall glasses of iced sweet tea.

1. Place chicken in a resealable plastic bag set in a shallow dish. Pour hot pepper sauce over chicken. Seal bag; turn to coat. Marinate in the refrigerator 1 to 24 hours, turning bag occasionally.

2. Drain chicken, discarding marinade. In another large resealable plastic bag combine flour, cornmeal, and salt. Add chicken drumsticks, a few at a time, shaking to coat.

3. Meanwhile, in a 12-inch heavy skillet heat ½ inch oil over medium-high heat to 350°F. Reduce heat to medium. Carefully add chicken to skillet. Cook 25 to 30 minutes or until chicken is done (170°F), turning occasionally to brown evenly. Drain on paper towels. If desired, serve with grilled mini sweet peppers and drizzle with additional hot sauce.

PER SERVING *164 cal., 11 g fat (2 g sat. fat), 38 mg chol., 203 mg sodium, 5 g carb., 0 g fiber, 11 g pro.*

PREP 15 minutes
MARINATE 1 hour   **COOK** 25 minutes

8 servings	ingredients	16 servings
8	chicken drumsticks, skinned, if desired	16
¼ cup	hot pepper sauce	½ cup
⅓ cup	all-purpose flour	⅔ cup
2 Tbsp.	yellow cornmeal	¼ cup
½ tsp.	salt	1 tsp.
	Vegetable oil	
	Mini sweet peppers (optional)	

Chicken Caesar Salad with Parmesan Croutons

Enjoy this popular salad—a staple on restaurant menus everywhere—at home. Homemade croutons and dressing make it a cut above an ordinary toss-it-together weeknight salad.

1. For Parmesan Croutons, preheat oven to 300°F. Cut bread slices into 1-inch cubes. Pour melted butter into a large bowl. Stir in half the Parmesan cheese and the minced garlic. Add bread cubes, stirring to coat. Spread cubes in a single layer in a shallow baking pan or sheet. Bake 20 minutes or until crisp and golden brown. Cool completely.

2. Meanwhile, for dressing, in a blender combine lemon juice, anchovies, and garlic clove halves. Cover and blend until nearly smooth, stopping to scrape down sides as needed. Add oil, hard-cooked egg yolk, mustard, and sugar. Cover and blend until smooth.

3. In a large serving bowl combine lettuce, chicken, Parmesan Croutons, and, if desired, cherry tomatoes. Pour dressing over salad; toss gently to coat. Sprinkle with remaining Parmesan cheese; toss gently to combine. Season with black pepper.

PER SERVING *350 cal., 15 g fat (9 g sat. fat), 104 mg chol., 402 mg sodium, 15 g carb., 2 g fiber, 20 g pro.*

PREP 40 minutes
BAKE 20 minutes

6 servings	ingredients	12 servings
four ¾-inch slices	¾-inch slices Italian or French bread	eight ¾-inch slices
¼ cup	butter, melted	½ cup
¼ cup + 2 Tbsp.	grated Parmesan cheese	¾ cup
2	cloves garlic, minced	4
2 Tbsp.	lemon juice	¼ cup
3	anchovy fillets	6
3	cloves garlic, halved	6
¼ cup	olive oil	½ cup
1	hard-cooked egg yolk	2
1 tsp.	Dijon mustard	2 tsp.
½ tsp.	sugar	1 tsp.
10 cups	torn romaine lettuce	20 cups
2 cups	chopped cooked chicken	4 cups
⅔ cup	halved cherry tomatoes (optional)	1⅓ cups
	Freshly ground black pepper	

Chicken Enchilada Soup

It may seem strange to stir cornmeal into soup, but not only does the cornmeal give the soup texture and flavor, it also acts as a thickener.

1. In a 4-qt. Dutch oven heat oil over medium-high heat. Add onion and garlic; cook 4 minutes or until onion is tender, stirring occasionally. Stir in broth and cornmeal. Bring to boiling, stirring constantly. Stir in chicken, tomatoes, enchilada sauce, and chile peppers; heat through. Stir in half the cheese.

2. Top servings with remaining cheese and tortilla strips. If desired, serve with cilantro and/or sour cream and sprinkle with black pepper.

PER SERVING *286 cal., 14 g fat (5 g sat. fat), 52 mg chol., 781 mg sodium, 22 g carb., 3 g fiber, 18 g pro.*

START TO FINISH 35 minutes

8 servings	ingredients	16 servings
1 Tbsp.	vegetable oil	2 Tbsp.
1 cup	chopped onion	2 cups
2	cloves garlic, minced	4
one 32-oz. carton	reduced-sodium chicken broth	two 32-oz. cartons
½ cup	cornmeal	1 cup
2 cups	shredded cooked chicken	4 cups
one 14.5-oz. can	diced tomatoes, undrained	two 14.5-oz. cans
one 10-oz. can	enchilada sauce	two 10-oz. cans
one 4-oz. can	diced green chile peppers, undrained	two 4-oz. cans
1 cup	shredded cheddar cheese	2 cups
	Fried flour tortilla strips or tortilla chips	
	Snipped fresh cilantro and/or sour cream (optional)	
	Black pepper (optional)	

BBQ Chicken and Smoked Cheddar Sandwiches

Craving a tasty, toasty sandwich—now? Rotisserie chicken, packaged coleslaw mix, and preshredded cheese aid the effort in preparing these simple but very tasty sandwiches.

4 servings	ingredients	8 servings
1½ cups	shredded rotisserie chicken	3 cups
½ cup	coleslaw mix	1 cup
⅓ cup	barbecue sauce	⅔ cup
1 cup	shredded smoked cheddar or cheddar cheese	2 cups
8 slices	Texas toast or Italian bread	16 slices
	Nonstick cooking spray	

1. In a bowl combine chicken and coleslaw mix. Stir in barbecue sauce. Divide chicken mixture and cheese among four bread slices. Top with remaining bread slices. Lightly coat outsides of sandwiches with cooking spray.

2. Preheat a panini grill according to manufacturer's directions.* Place sandwiches, half or fewer at a time if necessary, in grill. Close lid and grill 2 to 3 minutes or until toasted and cheese is melted.

*TIP If you don't have a panini grill, use a nonstick grill pan or large nonstick skillet. If desired, weight sandwiches by putting another large heavy skillet on top. Cook until browned on bottoms, remove top skillet, turn sandwiches, and replace top skillet. Cook until bottoms are browned.

PER SERVING *429 cal., 16 g fat (7 g sat. fat), 77 mg chol., 968 mg sodium, 49 g carb., 2 g fiber, 25 g pro.*

Chicken-Spinach Calzones

These pocket pizzas freeze beautifully and are great to have on hand for a quick and satisfying supper. Fill, bake, and cool completely. Wrap the calzones individually in foil and freeze in resealable plastic bags. To reheat from frozen, place, still wrapped in foil, on a baking pan in a 375°F oven. Heat 20 minutes, then unwrap and heat 5 minutes to allow the crust to crisp slightly.

1. Preheat oven to 375°F. For the filling, in a large bowl combine chicken, spinach, and pizza cheese. Stir in ¼ cup of the pizza sauce.

2. On a lightly floured surface, roll pizza dough to a 12-inch square. Cut into four 6-inch squares.

3. Place about ⅔ cup of the filling onto half of each dough square about ½ inch from edge. Moisten edges with water and fold over, forming a triangle or rectangle. Pinch or press with a fork to seal edges. Using the tip of a knife, cut small slits into tops of dough; place on an ungreased baking sheet.

4. Brush tops of calzones with milk and, if desired, sprinkle with Parmesan cheese. Bake 18 minutes or until calzones are golden brown and heated through. In a small saucepan heat the remaining pizza sauce; serve with calzones.

FOR 8 SERVINGS In Step 1, use ½ cup of the pizza sauce. In Step 2, cut a total of eight 6-inch squares.

PER SERVING *295 cal., 9 g fat (3 g sat. fat), 35 mg chol., 1,221 mg sodium, 31 g carb., 1 g fiber, 22 g pro.*

PREP 30 minutes
BAKE 18 minutes

4 servings	ingredients	8 servings
1½ cups	chopped cooked chicken	3 cups
1¼ cups	chopped fresh spinach	2½ cups
¾ cup	shredded pizza cheese	1½ cups
half 14- to 15-oz. jar	pizza sauce	one 14- to 15-oz. jar
one 13.8-oz. pkg.	refrigerated pizza dough	two 13.8-oz. pkg.
	Milk	
	Finely shredded Parmesan or Romano cheese (optional)	

Pesto Chicken Penne

Prepared pesto comes in both shelf-stable jars and in plastic tubs in the refrigerated section. If you can find the refrigerated version, it has better flavor and much brighter green color than jarred pesto.

START TO FINISH 20 minutes

4 servings	ingredients	8 servings
4 cups	dried penne, mostaccioli, or bow tie pasta	8 cups
2 cups	broccoli florets	4 cups
one 7-oz. container	basil pesto	two 7-oz. containers
2½ cups	coarsely chopped rotisserie chicken	5 cups
one 7-oz. jar	roasted red sweet peppers, drained and cut into strips	two 7-oz. jars
¼ cup	finely shredded Parmesan cheese	½ cup
½ tsp.	coarsely ground black pepper	1 tsp.

1. Cook pasta according to package directions, adding broccoli the last 2 minutes of cooking. Drain, reserving ½ cup pasta water; set aside. Return drained pasta and broccoli to saucepan.

2. Stir together pesto and the reserved pasta water. Add pesto mixture, chicken, and roasted peppers to pasta in saucepan. Stir gently to mix. Cook over medium heat until heated through. Stir in Parmesan cheese.

3. Top servings with additional Parmesan cheese, if desired, and sprinkle with black pepper.

FOR 8 SERVINGS In Step 1, reserve 1 cup pasta water.

PER SERVING *672 cal., 35 g fat (7 g sat. fat), 93 mg chol., 857 mg sodium, 53 g carb., 3 g fiber, 37 g pro.*

Chicken, Prosciutto, and Gorgonzola Risotto

Risotto takes a bit of standing and stirring, but the rich, velvety result is well worth the effort. Arborio rice—a short-grained rice with a relatively high starch content—helps to create the creamy texture.

1. In a large saucepan cook onion and garlic in hot oil over medium heat 3 to 5 minutes or until onion is tender, stirring occasionally. Add rice; cook 3 to 5 minutes or until rice is golden, stirring frequently.

2. Meanwhile, in a medium saucepan bring broth to boiling; reduce heat. Cover and keep broth simmering. Carefully stir ½ cup of the broth into rice mixture. Cook over medium heat until broth is absorbed, stirring frequently. Continue adding broth, ½ cup at a time, stirring frequently until broth has been absorbed. Stir chicken and prosciutto into rice with final ½ cup broth. Rice should be tender and creamy (this should take 20 to 25 minutes).

3. Top servings with cheese and, if desired, lemon zest and/or fresh thyme.

*TIP To substitute ½ cup dry white wine for ½ cup of the broth, gently heat the wine separately and stir it into the rice as the first ½ cup of liquid.

PER SERVING *286 cal., 10 g fat (2 g sat. fat), 62 mg chol., 685 mg sodium, 28 g carb., 1 g fiber, 21 g pro.*

START TO FINISH 40 minutes

6 servings	ingredients	12 servings
½ cup	chopped onion	1 cup
2	cloves garlic, minced	4
2 Tbsp.	olive oil	¼ cup
1 cup	uncooked Arborio rice	2 cups
two 14.5-oz. cans	reduced-sodium chicken broth*	four 14.5-oz. cans
1 cup	coarsely shredded rotisserie chicken	2 cups
¼ cup	bite-size strips prosciutto	½ cup
2 Tbsp.	crumbled Gorgonzola or other blue cheese	¼ cup
	Lemon zest (optional)	
	Fresh thyme (optional)	

Southwestern Chicken and Macaroni Salad

A hit of salsa is a quick and easy way to bring flavor to this crowd-pleasing dish. Use any kind of salsa you like—tomato-based, salsa verde (tomatillo-based), mild, medium, or hot.

PREP 35 minutes
ROAST 20 minutes

5 servings	ingredients	10 servings
1	poblano chile peppers, halved lengthwise and seeded (tip, page 15)	2
half 25-oz. pkg.	frozen cooked crispy chicken strips	one 25-oz. pkg.
4 oz.	dried elbow macaroni	8 oz.
2 oz.	cream cheese, softened	4 oz.
⅓ cup	salsa	⅔ cup
½	avocado, halved, seeded, peeled, and chopped	1

1. Preheat oven to 450°F. Line a baking sheet with foil. Place peppers, cut sides down, on the prepared baking sheet. Roast 20 minutes or until peppers are charred and very tender. Bring foil up around peppers and fold edges together to enclose. Let stand 15 minutes or until cool enough to handle. Peel off and discard skins; chop peppers.

2. Meanwhile, cook chicken and macaroni separately according to package directions. Drain macaroni; rinse with cold water and drain again. Cut chicken into ½-inch pieces.

3. In a large bowl beat cream cheese and half the salsa on low until smooth. Gradually beat in the remaining salsa. Stir in roasted peppers and macaroni. Gently fold in chicken and avocado.

PER SERVING *312 cal., 14 g fat (4 g sat. fat), 37 mg chol., 600 mg sodium, 30 g carb., 3 g fiber, 17 g pro.*

Turkey and Mango Salad with Chutney Vinaigrette

The simplest way to prepare a mango is to stand it upright on a cutting board and slice down, top to bottom, as closely as you can on either side of the large seed. Place each half, round side down, on the cutting board and cut it to (but not through) the skin in a cross-hatch pattern. Press the flesh inside out and cut off the diced fruit.

1. For rub, in a small bowl stir together first six ingredients (through cayenne pepper). Cut turkey in half horizontally to make two steaks. Sprinkle rub over both sides of the turkey; rub in with your fingers.

2. In a large skillet cook turkey in hot oil over medium heat 6 to 8 minutes or until no longer pink (170°F), turning once. Transfer turkey to a cutting board; thinly slice.

3. Meanwhile, for the Chutney Vinaigrette, in a small bowl stir together the chutney, oil, and vinegar.

4. In a large bowl combine spinach, red onion, pea pods, mango, and Chutney Vinaigrette; toss to coat. Divide salad among serving plates; arrange turkey slices on top. Sprinkle with pumpkin seeds.

PER SERVING *308 cal., 9 g fat (1 g sat. fat), 53 mg chol., 426 mg sodium, 29 g carb., 4 g fiber, 26 g pro.*

START TO FINISH 25 minutes

4 servings	ingredients	8 servings
1 tsp.	ground coriander	2 tsp.
1 tsp.	ground cumin	2 tsp.
¼ tsp.	salt	½ tsp.
¼ tsp.	ground ginger	½ tsp.
¼ tsp.	black pepper	½ tsp.
⅛ tsp.	cayenne pepper	¼ tsp.
one 12-oz.	turkey breast tenderloin	two 12-oz.
2 tsp.	canola oil	4 tsp.
¼ cup	mango chutney, large pieces snipped	½ cup
1 Tbsp.	canola oil	2 Tbsp.
4½ tsp.	rice vinegar	3 Tbsp.
6 cups	fresh baby spinach	12 cups
¼	medium red onion, thinly sliced	½
1 cup	fresh snow pea pods, trimmed	2 cups
1	mango, seeded, peeled, and cubed	2
2 Tbsp.	roasted pumpkin seeds (pepitas) (tip, page 8)	¼ cup

Turkey Peanut Stew

This rich, creamy, and slightly sweet stew is inspired by a peanut soup that is popular in West Africa. Bump up the amount of crushed red pepper if you like more heat—or serve with a vinegary hot sauce on the side.

PREP 35 minutes
COOK 15 minutes

4 servings	ingredients	8 servings
3	green onions, whites and green parts separated, thinly sliced	6
½	green sweet pepper, seeded and cut into 1-inch pieces	1
½ tsp.	coconut or canola oil	1 tsp.
1½ Tbsp.	finely chopped fresh ginger	3 Tbsp.
2	cloves garlic, minced	4
1 tsp.	ground coriander	2 tsp.
1 tsp.	ground cumin	2 tsp.
½ tsp.	crushed red pepper	1 tsp.
½ tsp.	salt	1 tsp.
½ tsp.	black pepper	1 tsp.
one + half 14.5-oz. cans	reduced-sodium chicken broth	three 14.5-oz. cans
1 cup	cubed, peeled sweet potato	2 cups
½ cup	creamy peanut butter	1 cup
2½ Tbsp.	tomato paste	5 Tbsp.
1½ cups	shredded cooked turkey	3 cups
half 14.5-oz. can	diced tomatoes, undrained	one 14.5-oz. can
⅓ cup	chopped fresh cilantro	⅔ cup
¾ cup	chopped lightly salted peanuts	1½ cups

1. In a 3-qt. saucepan cook white parts of green onions and sweet pepper in hot oil 5 minutes, stirring occasionally. Add next seven ingredients (through black pepper). Cook and stir 30 seconds. Add broth and sweet potato. Bring to boiling; reduce heat. Simmer, covered, 10 to 15 minutes or until potato is tender.

2. Ladle about ½ cup hot broth into a medium bowl. Whisk in peanut butter until smooth. Whisk in tomato paste.

3. Add turkey, peanut butter mixture, and tomatoes to saucepan. Cook, covered, over medium-low heat 5 minutes, stirring occasionally. Stir in cilantro. Top with green onion slices and peanuts.

FOR 8 SERVINGS In Step 1, use a 4- to 6-qt. Dutch oven. In Step 2, use 1 cup hot broth.

PER SERVING *446 cal., 27 g fat (6 g sat. fat), 53 mg chol., 1,094 mg sodium, 27 g carb., 6 g fiber, 30 g pro.*

Turkey Lettuce Wraps with Spicy Peanut Sauce

These crisp, light, and low-carb wraps can be seasoned with either Chinese five-spice powder (cinnamon, cloves, fennel seeds, star anise, and Szechuan peppercorns) or curry powder.

PREP 15 minutes
COOK 20 minutes

4 servings	ingredients	8 servings
1 lb.	ground uncooked turkey	2 lb.
3	cloves garlic, minced	6
1 Tbsp.	grated fresh ginger	2 Tbsp.
1 tsp.	five-spice powder or curry powder	2 tsp.
¼ cup	sugar	½ cup
¼ cup	crunchy peanut butter	½ cup
2 Tbsp.	water	¼ cup
1 Tbsp.	vegetable oil	2 Tbsp.
	Sriracha sauce	
2 cups	coarsely shredded broccoli* or purchased broccoli slaw	4 cups
1	small red onion, thinly sliced	2
	Salt and black pepper	
8	large Boston lettuce leaves	16
8	lime wedges	16
	Snipped fresh cilantro (optional)	

1. In a large nonstick skillet cook turkey over medium-high heat 5 minutes, stirring occasionally. Stir in garlic, ginger, and half the five-spice powder; cook 5 minutes more or until turkey is no longer pink. Using a slotted spoon transfer turkey mixture to a bowl; set aside. Wipe out skillet.

2. For the Spicy Peanut Sauce, in a saucepan stir together sugar, peanut butter, water, and oil. Cook and stir over medium-low heat just until bubbly and sugar is dissolved. Season to taste with sriracha sauce. Set aside.

3. In the same skillet cook broccoli, onion, and remaining five-spice powder 4 minutes or just until broccoli and onion are tender. Stir in the turkey mixture; heat through. Season to taste with salt and pepper.

4. Spoon about 1 tbsp Spicy Peanut Sauce on each lettuce leaf. Divide turkey-broccoli filling among lettuce leaves. Squeeze lime juice over each. If desired, sprinkle with cilantro.

*TIP Shred broccoli in a food processor with a coarse shredding blade or a handheld box shredder. If broccoli stalks are tough, peel them before shredding.

PER SERVING *210 cal., 13 g fat (3 g sat. fat), 44 mg chol., 160 mg sodium, 12 g carb., 2 g fiber, 13 g pro.*

Savory Stromboli Cups

Stromboli is yet another ingenious and delicious Italian combination of bread, tomato sauce, cheese, and meat. Traditional stromboli is usually a large spiraled loaf that is baked and sliced. These miniature versions made in muffin cups make fun party food and are sure to appeal to kids too!

1. Preheat oven to 375°F. Generously coat twelve 2½-inch muffin cups with cooking spray.

2. On a lightly floured surface, roll pizza dough into a 12×10-inch rectangle. Spread with pizza sauce; sprinkle with sweet pepper. Top with turkey and capicola slices; sprinkle with 1 cup of the cheese.

3. Starting from a long side, roll up dough rectangle. Pinch dough to seal seams. Slice roll into 12 pieces and arrange in prepared muffin cups.

4. Bake 15 minutes. Sprinkle with remaining cheese. Bake 5 minutes more or until dough is golden and cheese is melted. Cool in muffin cups on a wire rack 5 minutes. Remove from muffin cups. If desired, serve with additional pizza sauce.

FOR 12 SERVINGS In Step 1, use two 12-cup muffin pans. In Step 2, use 2 cups of the cheese.

PER SERVING *327 cal., 12 g fat (5 g sat. fat), 31 mg chol., 899 mg sodium, 34 g carb., 3 g fiber, 18 g pro.*

PREP 25 minutes
BAKE 20 minutes   **COOL** 5 minutes

6 servings	ingredients	12 servings
	Nonstick cooking spray	
one 13.8-oz. pkg.	refrigerated pizza dough with whole grain	two 13.8-oz. pkg.
½ cup	pizza sauce	1 cup
½ cup	chopped green sweet pepper	1 cup
3 oz.	thin slices deli-style turkey breast	6 oz.
3 oz.	thin slices deli-style capicola	6 oz.
1½ cups	shredded Italian cheese blend	3 cups

CHAPTER 3

Meat

These recipes featuring beef, pork, and lamb and a world of flavors—from a sweet and spicy Thai salad to an Italian skillet—will satisfy the heartiest appetites.

72

97

103

Beef and Bean Burritos

After more than two hours of simmering in liquid seasoned with smoky chipotle peppers, chili powder, and garlic salt, the beef chuck roast is butter-knife tender and flavorful.

PREP 1 hour
COOK 2 hours 15 minutes

6 servings	ingredients	12 servings
1 lb.	boneless beef chuck roast, trimmed and cut into 2-inch pieces	2 lb.
2 tsp.	chipotle peppers in adobo sauce, chopped (tip, page 15)	4 tsp.
1 tsp.	chili powder	2 tsp.
½ tsp.	garlic salt	1 tsp.
1 Tbsp.	canola oil	2 Tbsp.
¾ cup	water	1½ cups
⅔ cup	water	1⅓ cups
⅓ cup	brown rice	⅔ cup
2 Tbsp.	snipped fresh cilantro	¼ cup
2 Tbsp.	fresh lime or lemon juice	¼ cup
6	8-inch whole wheat flour tortillas, warmed	12
1½ cups	shredded fresh spinach	3 cups
1 cup	pico de gallo	2 cups
¾ cup	seasoned black beans, drained and warmed	1½ cups
¾ cup	reduced-fat shredded Mexican-style four-cheese blend	1½ cups
¾ cup	guacamole or mashed avocado	1½ cups

1. In a bowl combine first four ingredients (through garlic salt); toss to coat.

2. In a large saucepan heat oil over medium-high heat. Add beef mixture, half at a time. Cook 5 minutes or until beef is browned, stirring occasionally. Return all beef to the pan. Add ¾ water. Bring to boiling; reduce heat. Simmer, covered, 2¼ hours or until beef is fork-tender.

3. Meanwhile, for the rice, in a saucepan combine ⅔ water and rice. Bring to boiling; reduce heat. Cook, covered, 40 to 45 minutes or until rice is tender and liquid is absorbed. Stir in cilantro and lime juice.

4. Transfer beef to a bowl. Shred beef using two forks. Add some of the cooking liquid, if needed, to moisten the meat. Keep warm.

5. Lay tortillas on a flat work surface. Spoon rice along the bottom one-third of the tortillas. Top with beef and remaining ingredients. Fold bottoms of tortillas over filling. Fold in sides. Roll up tortillas tightly. Cut burritos in half.

PER SERVING *385 cal., 17 g fat (4 g sat. fat), 58 mg chol., 915 mg sodium, 39 g carb., 17 g fiber, 32 g pro.*

Philly Cheesesteak Burritos

Partially freezing the meat before slicing firms it up and allows you to cut thinner slices than if you tried to slice it right out of the refrigerator.

PREP 40 minutes
FREEZE 30 minutes

4 servings	ingredients	8 servings
1 lb.	beef top round steak, trimmed	2 lb.
2 tsp.	all-purpose flour	4 tsp.
¼ tsp.	dry mustard	½ tsp.
½ cup	fat-free or 2% milk	1 cup
1 oz.	Provolone cheese, torn into pieces	2 oz.
2 Tbsp.	grated Parmesan cheese	¼ cup
1 tsp.	olive oil	2 tsp.
one 8-oz. pkg.	sliced button or cremini mushrooms	two 8-oz. pkg.
1	large onion, thinly sliced	2
1	red sweet pepper, cut into thin slices	2
½ to 1 tsp.	bottled hot pepper sauce	1 to 2 tsp.
4	8- to 9-inch whole wheat flour tortillas	8

1. Freeze meat 30 minutes. Thinly slice across the grain into bite-size strips.

2. For the cheese sauce, in a saucepan combine flour and dry mustard. Gradually add milk, stirring with a whisk until blended. Cook and stir until mixture comes to boiling; reduce heat. Cook and stir 1 minute or until slightly thickened. Gradually add cheeses, stirring until smooth. Remove from heat; cover and keep warm. Sauce will thicken as it cools.

3. In an extra-large skillet heat oil over medium-high heat. Add half the meat; cook and stir 3 minutes or until slightly pink in center. Remove with a slotted spoon. Repeat with remaining meat; remove. Add mushrooms, onion, and sweet pepper to skillet; cook and stir 4 minutes or just until tender. Return meat to skillet. Season with hot pepper sauce.

4. Spoon about 1¼ cups filling onto each tortilla. Top with about 2 Tbsp. cheese sauce. Fold bottom edge of tortilla up and over filling. Fold one opposite side in; roll up from the bottom.

FOR 8 SERVINGS In Step 3, use a 4-qt. Dutch oven.

PER SERVING *329 cal., 11 g fat (3 g sat. fat), 65 mg chol., 488 mg sodium, 31 g carb., 14 g fiber, 39 g pro.*

Jalapeño Steak Sandwiches

Scoring the meat before marinating it allows the flavors of the marinade—lime, Dijon, jalapeño, and garlic—to more deeply penetrate it.

1. Score both sides of meat in a diamond pattern by making shallow diagonal cuts at 1-inch intervals. Place meat in a resealable plastic bag set in a shallow dish.

2. For marinade, in a small bowl whisk together oil, lime juice, mustard, jalapeños, garlic, and salt. Pour marinade over meat. Seal bag; turn to coat meat. Marinate in refrigerator 4 to 24 hours.

3. Drain meat, discarding marinade. Heat a large nonstick or well-seasoned grill pan over medium heat. Add meat, in batches if necessary; cook 14 to 16 minutes or until medium (160°F), turning once. Thinly slice meat diagonally across the grain.

4. Spread toasted bread slices with mayonnaise. Layer meat, onion, cheese, and cilantro between bread slices. If desired, serve with lime wedges.

***TIP** Or for 6 servings, use ½ cup mayonnaise plus 1 tsp. chili powder. For 12 servings use 1 cup mayonnaise and 2 tsp. chili powder.

FOR 12 SERVINGS In Step 1, use two plastic bags for meat and marinade.

PER SERVING *560 cal., 28 g fat (6 g sat. fat), 158 mg chol., 965 mg sodium, 46 g carb., 0 g fiber, 36 g pro.*

PREP 25 minutes
MARINATE 4 hours   **COOK** 14 minutes

6 servings	ingredients	12 servings
1¼ to 1½ lb.	beef flank steak, trimmed	2½ to 3 lb.
⅓ cup	olive oil	⅔ cup
⅓ cup	lime juice	⅔ cup
3 Tbsp.	Dijon mustard	¼ cup + 2 Tbsp.
3	jalapeños, finely chopped (tip, page 15)	6
3	cloves garlic, minced	6
1 tsp.	kosher salt	2 tsp.
12 slices	Texas toast or other thick-cut white bread, toasted	24 slices
½ cup	chipotle mayonnaise*	1 cup
1	medium red onion, quartered and thinly sliced	2
1 cup (4 oz.)	queso fresco, crumbled, or farmer cheese	2 cups (8 oz.)
	Fresh cilantro sprigs	
	Lime wedges (optional)	

Grilled Steak and Onion Salad with Blue Cheese Toast

Grilled red onions are whirled in a blender with cider vinegar, olive oil, salt, pepper, and a little sugar to create a unique vinaigrette for this steakhouse-style salad.

START TO FINISH 25 minutes

4 servings	ingredients	8 servings
4	1-inch slices crusty bread	8
2 to 3 oz.	blue cheese, cut into 4 wedges	4 to 6 oz.
2	small red onions, cut into wedges	4
¼ cup + 2 Tbsp.	olive oil	¾ cup
1 lb.	boneless beef breakfast steak, thin cut	2 lb.
¾ tsp.	salt	1½ tsp.
¾ tsp.	black pepper	1½ tsp.
¼ cup	cider vinegar	½ cup
1 tsp.	sugar	2 tsp.
2	hearts of romaine lettuce, halved	4
	Fresh basil leaves (optional)	

1. Grill bread on the grill rack directly over medium heat 2 minutes or until toasted, turning once. Top each slice with a cheese wedge; set aside.

2. Brush onion wedges with 2 Tbsp. of the oil. Grill 1 to 2 minutes on each side; move to side of grill. Sprinkle steaks with ¼ tsp. each salt and pepper. Place on grill rack over heat. Cover and grill 4 minutes or until desired doneness, turning once.

3. Meanwhile, for vinaigrette, in a blender or food processor combine one-third of the grilled onions, the vinegar, sugar, and remaining salt and pepper. Cover and blend until smooth. With blender or processor running, add remaining oil through opening in lid.

4. Serve steak, the remaining grilled onions, and blue cheese toast on romaine leaves. Sprinkle with basil, if desired. Pass vinaigrette.

FOR 8 SERVINGS In Step 2, use 4 Tbsp. of the oil and ½ tsp. each salt and pepper.

PER SERVING *506 cal., 30 g fat (7 g sat. fat), 58 mg chol., 883 mg sodium, 25 g carb., 4 g fiber, 32 g pro.*

Beef and Bacon Chili

You can use either beef stew meat or ground beef in this hearty chili. The texture will be different depending on which way you go, but the savory stew of meat, tomatoes, and beans flavored with garlic, chili powder, and smoky bacon will be the same.

1. In a 4- to 6-qt. Dutch oven cook chopped bacon and beef, half at a time, over medium heat until beef is browned. Drain off fat. Reduce heat; add onion and half the minced garlic. Cook and stir until onion is tender.

2. Add tomatoes, beans, and half the chili powder. Bring to boiling; reduce heat. Simmer, covered, 1 hour, stirring occasionally. Stir in remaining garlic, remaining chili powder, and vinegar. Cook, covered, 1 hour. If necessary, stir in water to make desired consistency. Serve with shredded cheese, crumbled bacon, and, if desired, fresh oregano.

PER SERVING *546 cal., 23 g fat (9 g sat. fat), 107 mg chol., 1,222 mg sodium, 31 g carb., 8 g fiber, 54 g pro.*

PREP 30 minutes
COOK 2 hours

6 servings	ingredients	12 servings
4 slices	bacon, chopped	8 slices
3 lb.	beef stew meat or ground beef	6 lb.
1	large onion, cut into ½-inch slices	2
4	cloves garlic, minced	8
two 28-oz. cans	whole tomatoes, undrained	four 28-oz. cans
one 15.5-oz. can	navy beans, rinsed and drained	two 15.5-oz. cans
one 15.5-oz. can	red beans, rinsed and drained	two 15.5-oz. cans
2 Tbsp.	chili powder	¼ cup
2 Tbsp.	red wine vinegar	¼ cup
	Shredded cheddar or Mexican-style four-cheese blend	
	Cooked bacon, crumbled	
	Snipped fresh oregano (optional)	

Baby Beet and Flank Steak Dijon

PREP 30 minutes
ROAST 1 hour   GRILL 17 minutes

6 servings	ingredients	12 servings
2½ lb.	yellow and/or red baby beets, trimmed	5 lb.
one 1½ lb.	beef flank steak	two 1½ lb.
¾ tsp.	kosher salt	1½ tsp.
½ tsp.	coarse-ground black pepper	1 tsp.
¼ cup	stone-ground Dijon mustard	½ cup
1 Tbsp.	honey	2 Tbsp.
⅓ cup	finely chopped shallots	⅔ cup
¼ cup	olive oil	½ cup
2 Tbsp.	white wine vinegar	¼ cup
6	¼-inch slices French bread	12
2 Tbsp.	olive oil	¼ cup
2 Tbsp.	Parmesan cheese	¼ cup
¼ cup	snipped fresh Italian parsley	½ cup

For an eye-catching color combination, use a mix of beets—yellow, red, and even the candy cane-striped variety called Chioggia beets.

1. Preheat oven to 375°F. Tightly wrap beets in foil, wrapping each color separately. Roast beets 1 to 1¼ hours or until tender; cool. Peel beets; cut into ¼-inch slices. Chill until needed.

2. Meanwhile, trim fat from meat. Score both sides of meat in a diamond pattern by making shallow diagonal cuts at 1-inch intervals. Sprinkle meat with salt and half the pepper. In a small bowl stir together 1 Tbsp. mustard and the honey; spread over meat.

3. Grill meat, covered, directly over medium heat 17 to 21 minutes for medium (160°F), turning once. Transfer to a cutting board. Cut meat across the grain into ¼-inch slices; halve or quarter long slices.

4. For dressing, in a screw-top jar combine shallots, oil, vinegar, remaining pepper, and remaining mustard. Cover and shake well.

5. Meanwhile, brush both sides of bread with olive oil and sprinkle lightly with additional kosher salt and coarse ground black pepper. Place on a baking sheet. Bake 10 to 12 minutes or until golden, turning once.

6. Sprinkle toasted bread with Parmesan cheese. Drizzle with some of the dressing. Top with meat and beet slices; drizzle with the remaining dressing. Sprinkle with parsley.

FOR 12 SERVINGS In Step 2, use 2 Tbsp. mustard.

PER SERVING *469 cal., 21 g fat (5 g sat. fat), 70 mg chol., 872 mg sodium, 37 g carb., 5 g fiber, 31 g pro.*

Thai Rice Noodle and Grilled Steak Salad

This salad is a riot of tastes, textures, and temperatures. A marinade and dressing infused with tangy, slightly sweet and spicy flavors spark the combination of crisp and cool greens, veggies, and herbs with warm steak off of the grill.

1. For marinade, remove zest from two of the limes; juice to yield ¼ cup. Set aside. In a small bowl whisk together 1 Tbsp. of the fish sauce, half the brown sugar, the lime zest, oil, and garlic. Place steak in a resealable plastic bag; pour marinade over steak. Seal bag, turning to coat. Marinate in refrigerator 15 minutes or up to 24 hours. Drain; discard marinade.

2. Grill steak, covered, over medium heat 15 to 18 minutes or until desired doneness. Cover. Let rest 5 minutes.

3. Meanwhile, for dressing, whisk together lime juice, remaining fish sauce, remaining brown sugar, 1 Tbsp. water, and the crushed red pepper.

4. Cut remaining lime in wedges. In a large bowl combine noodles, lettuce, cucumber, carrots, basil, and mint. Thinly slice steak against the grain; arrange on salad. If desired, sprinkle with peanuts. Serve with dressing and lime wedges.

FOR 8 SERVINGS In Step 1, remove zest from four of the limes; juice to yield ½ cup. Use 2 Tbsp. of the fish sauce. In Step 3, use 2 Tbsp. water.

PER SERVING *400 cal., 9 g fat (3 g sat. fat), 55 mg chol., 927 mg sodium, 56 g carb., 3 g fiber, 22 g pro.*

PREP 20 minutes   **MARINATE** 15 minutes
GRILL 15 minutes   **REST** 5 minutes

4 servings	ingredients	8 servings
3	limes	6
3 Tbsp.	fish sauce	¼ cup + 2 Tbsp.
1 Tbsp.	packed brown sugar	2 Tbsp.
1 Tbsp.	vegetable oil	2 Tbsp.
2	cloves garlic, minced	4
12 oz.	beef shoulder top blade, flank, or skirt steak, trimmed	1½ lb.
1 Tbsp.	water	2 Tbsp.
¼ tsp.	crushed red pepper	½ tsp.
8 oz.	dried flat rice noodles, cooked according to pkg. directions	16 oz.
2 cups	torn romaine or green leaf lettuce	4 cups
1¾ cups	thinly sliced seedless cucumber	3½ cups
1 cup	thinly bias-sliced carrots	2 cups
½ cup	fresh basil leaves	1 cup
⅓ cup	fresh mint leaves	⅔ cup
½ cup	peanuts, coarsely chopped (optional)	1 cup

Grilled Meat Loaf Burgers

A combination of meats—beef with either pork or lamb—gives these burgers a rich dimension of flavor that a single meat would not.

1. In a large bowl combine egg, chopped onion, panko, half the peach preserves, the Worcestershire sauce, oregano, and pepper. Add ground beef and ground pork; mix well. Shape meat mixture into four ¾-inch-thick patties.

2. Grill patties on the rack of a covered grill directly over medium heat 14 to 18 minutes or until done (165°F), turning once and spreading with remaining peach preserves halfway through grilling. If desired, top with onion slices and cheese, then grill 1 minute more or until melted.

3. Serve patties on buns with barbecue sauce, and, if desired, sprinkle with chopped parsley.

FOR 8 SERVINGS In Step 1, shape meat mixture into eight ¾-inch thick patties

PER SERVING *519 cal., 24 g fat (8 g sat. fat), 125 mg chol., 438 mg sodium, 47 g carb., 2 g fiber, 28 g pro.*

START TO FINISH 30 minutes

4 servings	ingredients	8 servings
1	egg, lightly beaten	2
¼ cup	finely chopped red onion	½ cup
¼ cup	panko bread crumbs	½ cup
¼ cup	peach preserves	½ cup
1 Tbsp.	Worcestershire sauce	2 Tbsp.
½ tsp.	dried oregano, crushed	1 tsp.
¼ tsp.	black pepper	½ tsp.
8 oz.	ground beef	16 oz.
8 oz.	ground pork or ground lamb	16 oz.
	Red onion slices (optional)	
	Sliced cheddar cheese (optional)	
4	hamburger buns, split and toasted	8
	Barbecue sauce	
	Chopped fresh parsley (optional)	

Mini Gyro Burgers

These slider-size patties are flavored with mint, oregano, and red onion before they're broiled, tucked into a pita, and topped with refreshing tzatziki sauce.

PREP 20 minutes
BROIL 6 minutes

4 servings	ingredients	8 servings
8 oz.	ground lamb or beef	16 oz.
8 oz.	ground turkey	16 oz.
¼ cup	chopped fresh mint	½ cup
½ tsp.	dried oregano, crushed	1 tsp.
2 Tbsp.	finely chopped red onion	¼ cup
¼ tsp.	black pepper	½ tsp.
¾ tsp.	salt	1½ tsp.
1	small cucumber, peeled, seeded, and shredded	2
4	radishes, coarsely chopped	8
one 5.3-oz. container	plain Greek yogurt	two 5.3-oz. containers
1 Tbsp.	lemon juice	2 Tbsp.
1 Tbsp.	olive oil	2 Tbsp.
1 Tbsp.	snipped fresh mint	2 Tbsp.
1	clove garlic, minced	2
4	whole wheat or plain pita bread rounds	8

1. In a bowl combine the first six ingredients (through pepper) and ½ tsp. of the salt. Shape into eight ½-inch-thick patties; place on a foil-lined baking sheet. Broil 4 inches from heat 6 to 9 minutes or until done (165°F), turning once.

2. Meanwhile, for tzatziki cucumber sauce, in a bowl combine cucumber and radishes. In another bowl stir together yogurt, lemon juice, oil, mint, garlic, and remaining salt; gently stir into vegetables.

3. Place two patties on each pita; top with sauce. If desired, sprinkle with additional mint leaves.

FOR 8 SERVINGS In Step 1, use 1 tsp. of the salt. Shape into sixteen ½-inch-thick patties; place on two foil-lined baking sheets, broiling one sheet of patties at a time.

PER SERVING *468 cal., 22 g fat (9 g sat. fat), 92 mg chol., 790 mg sodium, 41 g carb., 5 g fiber, 28 g pro.*

Memphis Dry Ribs

Braising the ribs in apple juice in the oven 3 hours turns them meltingly tender before they're briefly smoked with hickory or oak wood chips in the grill. For added smokiness, use smoked paprika instead of sweet paprika.

1. Preheat oven to 275°F. Place ribs in a shallow roasting pan. In a bowl stir together next eight ingredients (through cayenne pepper). Remove 1 Tbsp. of the spice mixture for mop sauce; set aside. Sprinkle both sides of ribs with remaining spice mixture; rub in with your fingers.

2. Pour apple juice into pan around (not over) ribs. Bake, covered, 3 hours or until ribs are very tender. Remove from pan.

3. Meanwhile, soak 2 cups hickory or oak wood chips in water 1 hour. For mop sauce, in a bowl combine barbecue sauce and vinegar. Stir in reserved spice mixture.

4. Brush ribs generously with mop sauce. Prepare grill for indirect heat using a drip pan; add wood chips. Place ribs over drip pan. Grill, covered, over indirect medium heat 15 to 20 minutes or until heated through. If desired, serve ribs with additional barbecue sauce.

TO MAKE AHEAD Prepare as directed through Step 2. Cool ribs and wrap in foil. Place on a tray and chill up to 3 days. Transfer mop sauce to an airtight container and chill until needed. To serve, remove ribs from foil. Continue as directed in Step 3, except grill 20 to 25 minutes.

FOR 12 SERVINGS In Step 1, use two shallow roasting pans and set aside 2 Tbsp. of spice mixture for mop sauce.

PER SERVING *487 cal., 29 g fat (11 g sat. fat), 129 mg chol., 809 mg sodium, 18 g carb., 1 g fiber, 37 g pro.*

PREP 25 minutes
BAKE 3 hours   **GRILL** 15 minutes

6 servings	ingredients	12 servings
4 lb.	meaty pork spareribs, trimmed	8 lb.
3 Tbsp.	packed brown sugar	¼ cup + 2 Tbsp.
2 Tbsp.	smoked or sweet paprika	¼ cup
2 tsp.	celery salt	4 tsp.
2 tsp.	onion powder	4 tsp.
1 tsp.	garlic powder	2 tsp.
1 tsp.	dried thyme, crushed	2 tsp.
1 tsp.	coarse-ground black pepper	2 tsp.
⅛ tsp.	cayenne pepper	¼ tsp.
½ cup	apple juice	1 cup
⅓ cup	barbecue sauce	⅔ cup
⅓ cup	cider vinegar	⅔ cup

Bahn Mi Noodle Bowl

This super-easy dish has all the flavors of bahn mi—a popular Vietnamese sandwich of sliced pork on a crisp baguette-style bun—but in a warming bowl of broth and noodles.

1. Cook noodles according to package directions (discard seasoning packets or reserve for another use); drain.

2. Coat a large skillet with cooking spray. Season pork with salt and pepper. Cook half the pork in skillet over medium-high heat 3 to 5 minutes or until browned. Using a slotted spoon, remove pork from skillet. Repeat with remaining pork. Stir in the next five ingredients (through ginger). Cook and stir until heated through. Stir in pork and cooked noodles. Spoon into shallow bowls. Top with radishes, cucumber, and cilantro.

PER SERVING *369 cal., 10 g fat (4 g sat. fat), 76 mg chol., 685 mg sodium, 36 g carb., 1 g fiber, 29 g pro.*

START TO FINISH 25 minutes

4 servings	ingredients	8 servings
two 3-oz. pkg.	ramen noodles (any flavor)	four 3-oz. pkg.
	Nonstick cooking spray	
1 lb.	pork tenderloin, trimmed and cut into bite-size pieces	2 lb.
	Salt and black pepper	
2 cups	chicken broth	4 cups
½ cup	rice vinegar	1 cup
2 Tbsp.	sriracha sauce	¼ cup
2 Tbsp.	sugar	¼ cup
½ tsp.	grated fresh ginger	1 tsp.
¼ cup	thinly sliced radishes	½ cup
¼ cup	thinly sliced English cucumber	½ cup
2 Tbsp.	snipped fresh cilantro	¼ cup

Pineapple-Pork Fried Rice

For best results, to make fried rice always use rice that has been cooked and chilled in the refrigerator (even overnight). The grains of cold rice separate better than those of warm or room temperature rice, which means they will incorporate more easily with the other ingredients.

1. In a small bowl combine egg and egg whites. Set aside. In a wok or extra-large skillet heat 2 tsp. of the oil over medium-high heat. Add meat, in batches if necessary; cook and stir 3 to 5 minutes or until slightly pink in center. Transfer meat to a bowl; cover to keep warm.

2. Add remaining oil to wok; heat over medium-high heat. Add pineapple, carrot, celery, green onions, and ginger; cook and stir 3 to 4 minutes or until vegetables are tender. Add garlic; cook and stir 30 seconds more.

3. Add egg mixture. Cook, without stirring, 5 to 10 seconds or until egg sets on bottom but remains runny on top. Add rice; cook 1 minute, turning and tossing constantly. Return cooked meat to wok; add peas, soy sauce, and cilantro. Cook and stir until heated through. If desired, serve with peanuts, lime wedges, and/or sriracha sauce.

FOR 8 SERVINGS In Step 1, use 4 tsp. of the oil.

PER SERVING *386 cal., 11 g fat (2 g sat. fat), 144 mg chol., 546 mg sodium, 41 g carb., 4 g fiber, 31 g pro.*

START TO FINISH 45 minutes

4 servings	ingredients	8 servings
1	egg, lightly beaten	2
2	egg whites	4
5 tsp.	vegetable oil	10 tsp.
1 lb.	pork tenderloin, trimmed, cut into bite-size pieces	2 lb.
1 cup	chopped fresh pineapple	2 cups
½ cup	thinly sliced carrot	1 cup
½ cup	thinly bias-sliced celery	1 cup
½ cup	sliced green onions	1 cup
2 tsp.	grated fresh ginger	4 tsp.
2	cloves garlic, minced	4
2 cups	cooked jasmine rice	4 cups
½ cup	frozen peas, thawed	1 cup
3 Tbsp.	reduced-sodium soy sauce	¼ cup + 2 Tbsp.
1 Tbsp.	snipped fresh cilantro	2 Tbsp.
	Finely chopped peanuts, lime wedges, and/or sriracha sauce (optional)	

Bacon-Wrapped Pork Tenderloin

Pork pairs very naturally with fruit. In this simple roast recipe, apricot or cherry preserves stirred together with a little vinegar makes a delicious glaze for brushing over the bacon-wrapped tenderloin.

1. Preheat oven to 425°F. Line a shallow roasting pan with foil. Place a rack in pan.

2. In a bowl stir together apricot preserves and vinegar. Lay bacon side by side on a work surface, overlapping slightly. Place tenderloin crosswise on bacon and roll up, wrapping bacon around tenderloin. Place tenderloin, bacon ends down, on rack in the prepared pan. Roast 20 minutes. Brush tenderloin with preserves mixture. Roast 5 to 10 minutes more or until bacon is crisp and pork is done (145°F). Remove from oven; let stand 3 minutes.

3. Meanwhile, in a large skillet heat oil over medium-high heat. Add green beans; cook and stir 3 to 5 minutes or just until crisp-tender. Add broth, honey, and salt. Cook and stir 3 minutes more or until liquid is nearly evaporated. Stir in almonds. Serve green beans with sliced tenderloin.

*TIP To toast nuts, preheat oven to 350°F. Spread nuts in a shallow baking pan. Bake 5 to 10 minutes or until nuts are light brown, shaking pan once or twice.

FOR 8 SERVINGS In Step 1, use two roasting pans, each with a rack in pan.

PER SERVING *392 cal., 15 g fat (4 g sat. fat), 93 mg chol., 575 mg sodium, 31 g carb., 2 g fiber, 33 g pro.*

PREP 20 minutes
ROAST 25 minutes   **STAND** 3 minutes

4 servings	ingredients	8 servings
⅓ cup	apricot or cherry preserves, large pieces chopped	⅔ cup
1 tsp.	red wine vinegar	2 tsp.
10 slices	bacon	20 slices
one 1-lb.	pork tenderloin, trimmed	two 1-lb.
1 Tbsp.	olive oil	2 Tbsp.
8 oz.	green beans, trimmed if desired	1 lb.
¼ cup	reduced-sodium chicken broth	½ cup
2 Tbsp.	honey	¼ cup
¼ tsp.	salt	½ tsp.
¼ cup	sliced almonds, toasted*	½ cup

Thai-Style Pork Salad

The fat in coconut milk tends to separate from the rest of the liquid as it sits in the can, which is why it's always a good idea before using coconut milk to pour it into a bowl and whisk thoroughly before measuring it.

1. In a large mixing bowl combine the first five ingredients (through ginger). Add pork; toss to coat and set aside.

2. Heat olive oil in an extra-large skillet over medium-high heat. Add meat mixture; cook 3 minutes. Add green beans; cook and stir 3 to 4 minutes or until crisp-tender and until pork is just slightly pink, stirring occasionally. Add carrots.

3. Spoon pork mixture onto cabbage leaves. Top with additional cilantro and serve with lime wedges.

*TIP Pour coconut milk into a bowl and whisk thoroughly before measuring.

PER SERVING *301 cal., 14 g fat (7 g sat. fat), 78 mg chol., 834 mg sodium, 14 g carb., 3 g fiber, 28 g pro.*

PREP 25 minutes
COOK 6 minutes

4 servings	ingredients	8 servings
half* 13.66 oz. can (¾ cup)	unsweetened coconut milk	one 13.66 oz. can
½ cup	snipped fresh cilantro	1 cup
⅓ cup	reduced-sodium soy sauce	⅔ cup
¼ cup	lime juice	½ cup
2 Tbsp.	grated fresh ginger	¼ cup
1 lb.	boneless pork loin, trimmed and cut into bite-size pieces	2 lb.
1 Tbsp.	olive oil	2 Tbsp.
1 cup	bias-sliced fresh green beans	2 cups
1 cup	shredded carrots	2 cups
	Napa cabbage leaves	
	Lime wedges	

Ginger Pork Chops with Curried Walnuts

The seasoned walnuts that serve as a topping for this autumnal skillet dish are so tasty you may want to make an extra batch for snacking.

1. In a large skillet cook and stir walnuts, curry powder, and cayenne in half the oil over medium heat 5 minutes; remove from skillet.

2. Add remaining oil to skillet. Add pork chops and onion. Cook 7 minutes or until pork is done (145°F), turning once.

3. Remove 1 Tbsp. zest and ¼ cup juice from orange. In a small bowl stir together orange zest and juice, soy sauce, honey, and ginger. Add to skillet along with butternut squash. Bring to boiling; heat through. Top with seasoned walnuts.

FOR 8 SERVINGS In Step 3, remove 2 Tbsp. zest and ½ cup juice from oranges. Cook pork chops in batches; cover to keep warm.

PER SERVING *508 cal., 30 g fat (4 g sat. fat), 79 mg chol., 678 mg sodium, 22 g carb., 5 g fiber, 41 g pro.*

START TO FINISH 40 minutes

4 servings	ingredients	8 servings
1 cup	walnuts	2 cups
½ tsp.	curry powder	1 tsp.
⅛ tsp.	cayenne pepper	¼ tsp.
2 Tbsp	vegetable oil	¼ cup
4	½-inch thick boneless pork chops	8
1	small red onion, cut into thin wedges	2
1	orange	2
¼ cup	reduced-sodium soy sauce	½ cup
1 Tbsp.	honey	2 Tbsp.
1 Tbsp.	grated fresh ginger	2 Tbsp.
2 cups	steamed butternut squash	4 cups

Bourbon-Sauced Pork Chops

You can use either boneless or bone-in chops in this recipe. In general, cooking meats on the bone helps to preserve their juiciness a bit, but for cuts that cook as quickly as these chops do it doesn't make a huge difference either way.

1. For sauce, in a small saucepan combine the first seven ingredients (through pepper). Bring to boiling; reduce heat. Simmer, uncovered, 10 minutes or until reduced to ½ cup. Stir together the water and cornstarch. Stir into bourbon mixture. Cook and stir until slightly thickened and bubbly; cook and stir 2 minutes more.

2. Grill chops, covered, directly over medium heat 14 to 16 minutes (145°F), turning once. Brush occasionally with sauce the last 5 minutes. If desired, serve chops with broccolini or mashed potatoes drizzled with any remaining sauce.

PER SERVING *558 cal., 23 g fat (8 g sat. fat), 193 mg chol., 575 mg sodium, 12 g carb., 0 g fiber, 60 g pro.*

PREP 15 minutes
COOK 10 minutes **GRILL** 14 minutes

4 servings	ingredients	8 servings
⅓ cup	bourbon or apple juice	⅔ cup
3 Tbsp.	reduced-sodium soy sauce	¼ cup + 2 Tbsp.
3 Tbsp.	packed brown sugar	¼ cup + 2 Tbsp.
2 Tbsp.	cider vinegar	¼ cup
2	cloves garlic, thinly sliced	4
½ tsp.	grated fresh ginger	1 tsp.
¼ tsp.	black pepper	½ tsp
1 Tbsp.	cold water	2 Tbsp.
½ tsp.	cornstarch	1 tsp.
4	pork chops, cut 1¼ inch thick	8
	Hot cooked broccolini or mashed potatoes (optional)	

Pork and Red Cabbage Skillet

Pork and red cabbage are a classic combination. While most red cabbage dishes have a sweet and sour flavor from a combination of sugar and vinegar, this simple skillet keeps it light and fresh with a splash of cider vinegar, salt, and quick-pickled red onions. Roasted and salted pepitas add crunch.

1. Place onion in a bowl with 1 Tbsp. vinegar and salt; stir well. Set aside.

2. In an extra-large skillet heat 1 Tbsp. of the oil over medium-high heat. Season pork with salt and black pepper to taste. Add half the pork to skillet. Cook 2 to 3 minutes on each side or until golden brown. Transfer to a plate; cover to keep warm. Repeat with remaining pork.

3. Add cabbage and remaining oil to skillet. Cook over medium 10 minutes or until wilted, stirring occasionally. Add onion mixture, remaining vinegar, and pepitas; toss to combine. Serve with pork.

*TIP If you can't find pork cutlets, cut two 8-oz. boneless pork loin chops in half crosswise. Place each piece between plastic wrap and, using a meat mallet, pound the pork to ¼-inch thickness. Cut each pounded piece in half crosswise for eight pieces total. For 16 pieces total, follow the same directions with four 8-oz. boneless pork loin chops.

FOR 8 SERVINGS In Step 1, use 2 Tbsp. of the vinegar. In Step 2, use 2 Tbsp. of oil.

PER SERVING *425 cal., 28 g fat (5 g sat. fat), 64 mg chol., 432 mg sodium, 12 g carb., 4 g fiber, 37 g pro.*

START TO FINISH 25 minutes

4 servings	ingredients	8 servings
1	medium red onion, thinly sliced	2
¼ cup	apple cider vinegar	½ cup
½ tsp.	salt	1 tsp.
3 Tbsp.	olive oil	¼ cup + 2 Tbsp.
8	2-oz. pork cutlets, pieces pounded ¼-inch thick*	16
	Black pepper	
4 cups	shredded red cabbage	8 cups
½ cup	roasted and salted pepitas	1 cup

Grilled Pork and Noodle Salad

If you want to avoid peeling and seeding the cucumber, look for an English (also called hothouse) cucumber. English cucumbers are long and thin and are usually wrapped in plastic to prevent them from drying out. They have thin, unwaxed skin that doesn't require peeling—and are considered seedless as well.

PREP 25 minutes
MARINATE 1 hour   **GRILL** 5 minutes

4 servings	ingredients	8 servings
3	boneless pork loin chops, cut ½ inch thick	6
½ cup	ginger vinaigrette or balsamic vinaigrette	1 cup
¾ tsp.	anise seeds, crushed	1½ tsp.
one 7-oz. pkg.	rice sticks	two 7-oz. pkg.
⅓ cup	vegetable oil	⅔ cup
2 cups	torn romaine lettuce	4 cups
1½ cups	thinly sliced peeled seeded cucumber	3 cups
½ cup	coarsely snipped fresh mint leaves	1 cup
½ cup	coarsely snipped fresh Thai basil or basil leaves	1 cup
½ cup	shredded carrot	1 cup
¼ cup	coarsely chopped peanuts	½ cup
	Thinly sliced cucumber	
	Fresh cilantro sprigs	
	Lime wedges	

1. Trim fat from chops. Place chops in a resealable plastic bag set in a shallow dish. For marinade, in a small bowl combine half the ginger vinaigrette and ¼ tsp. of the anise seeds. Pour marinade over chops in bag. Seal bag; turn to coat chops. Marinate in the refrigerator 1 to 4 hours, turning bag occasionally.

2. Cook rice sticks according to package directions; drain in a colander. Rinse with cold water until water runs clear; drain 20 minutes. Using kitchen scissors, snip rice sticks into 3- to 4-inch lengths. In a bowl combine rice sticks, oil, and remaining anise seeds; toss gently to coat. Set aside.

3. Drain chops, discarding marinade. Grill chops, covered, over medium heat 4 to 5 minutes (145°F), turning once. Remove chops from grill and let stand 3 minutes. Slice diagonally.

4. In another bowl combine lettuce, cucumber, mint, and basil. Pour the remaining ginger vinaigrette over salad; toss gently to coat.

5. Divide rice sticks among shallow bowls or dinner plates. Arrange lettuce and meat on top of rice sticks. Top with carrot, peanuts, additional cucumber, and cilantro. Serve with lime wedges.

FOR 8 SERVINGS In Step 1, use ½ tsp. anise seeds.

PER SERVING *618 cal., 37 g fat (6 g sat. fat), 35 mg chol., 428 mg sodium, 53 g carb., 3 g fiber, 19 g pro.*

Citrus Pork and Arugula Salad

Apricot season is sweet but fleeting—usually from about mid-May to late July. Late spring to midsummer sounds like a perfect time for this light and fresh pork and fruit salad. (If you want to make it outside of that time frame see the Tip, below.)

1. Trim fat from pork. Cut pork crosswise into ¼-inch slices. Sprinkle with salt and black pepper.

2. In an extra-large skillet cook pork, half at a time, in hot oil over medium-high heat 2 to 3 minutes or until meat is just slightly pink in center, turning once. Remove from skillet and set aside.

3. For dressing, in a screw-top jar combine orange zest and juice, vinegar, soy sauce, honey, sesame oil, and ginger. Cover and shake well to combine.

4. Place arugula on a serving platter. Top with pork slices, apricots, and avocado slices. Drizzle with the dressing.

*TIP If fresh apricots aren't available, for 4 servings use ¾ cup canned, unpeeled apricot halves in light syrup, drained and quartered. For 8 servings use 1½ cups canned, unpeeled apricot halves in light syrup, drained and quartered.

PER SERVING *272 cal., 11 g fat (2 g sat. fat), 74 mg chol., 314 mg sodium, 19 g carb., 3 g fiber, 26 g pro.*

START TO FINISH 30 minutes

4 servings	ingredients	8 servings
1 lb.	pork tenderloin	2 lb.
¼ tsp.	salt	½ tsp.
¼ tsp.	black pepper	½ tsp.
1 Tbsp.	canola oil	2 Tbsp.
½ tsp.	orange zest	1 tsp.
⅓ cup	orange juice	⅔ cup
1 Tbsp.	rice vinegar or white wine vinegar	2 Tbsp.
2 tsp.	reduced-sodium soy sauce	4 tsp.
2 tsp.	honey	4 tsp.
1 tsp.	toasted sesame oil	2 tsp.
½ tsp.	grated fresh ginger	1 tsp.
6 cups	baby arugula	12 cups
3	fresh* apricots, halved, seeded, and quartered	6
1	avocado, peeled, seeded, and sliced or chopped	2

Curried Pork Burgers

These knife-and-fork burgers get a double dose of curry—in the mayonnaise and in the meat mixture. Red cabbage leaves add a fresh crunch to every bite.

1. In a small bowl combine mayonnaise and ¼ tsp. curry powder; set aside. In a large bowl combine the next seven ingredients (through crushed red pepper), and remaining curry powder. Shape into four ¾-inch-thick patties. Lightly brush red onion slices with oil.

2. Grill patties, covered, directly over medium heat 14 to 18 minutes or until done (160°), turning once. Add red onion slices the last 8 minutes of grilling, turning once. Grill Texas toast slices 1 to 2 minutes per side or until toasted.

3. Place a cabbage leaf on each slice of Texas toast. Spread with mayonnaise mixture. Top with pork patties and some of the red onion slices.

FOR 8 SERVINGS In Step 1, use ½ tsp. curry powder.

PER SERVING *647 cal., 45 g fat (15 g sat. fat), 128 mg chol., 711 mg sodium, 28 g carb., 3 g fiber, 33 g pro.*

PREP 15 minutes
GRILL 14 minutes

4 servings	ingredients	8 servings
¼ cup	light mayonnaise	½ cup
1¼ tsp.	curry powder	2½ tsp.
1½ lb.	ground pork	3 lb.
¼ cup	finely chopped red onion	½ cup
3	cloves garlic, minced	6
1 tsp.	Worcestershire sauce	2 tsp.
½ tsp.	salt	1 tsp.
½ tsp.	black pepper	1 tsp.
¼ tsp.	crushed red pepper	½ tsp.
2	½-inch thick slices red onion	4
2 tsp.	olive oil	4 tsp.
4	slices Texas toast	8
4	red cabbage leaves	8
	Chopped fresh parsley (optional)	

Mexican Chorizo Noodle Bowl

You'll never use an entire can of chipotle peppers in a single recipe, but they freeze well for future use. Divide them into small portions and freeze in small plastic bags or containers.

START TO FINISH 40 minutes

6 servings	ingredients	12 servings
1 lb.	uncooked chorizo or hot Italian sausage	2 lb.
2	cloves garlic, minced	4
three 14.5-oz. cans	reduced-sodium chicken or vegetable broth	six 14.5-oz. cans
one 16-oz. jar	salsa	two 16-oz. jars
1 to 2	canned chipotle peppers in adobo sauce, drained and finely chopped	2 to 4
1 tsp.	dried oregano, crushed	2 tsp.
1 tsp.	ground cumin	2 tsp.
3 oz.	dried vermicelli or angel hair pasta, broken	6 oz.
1	small zucchini, cut up	2
1 cup	fresh or frozen whole kernel corn	2 cups
¼ cup	snipped fresh cilantro or Italian parsley (optional)	½ cup

1. Remove casing from chorizo, if present. Crumble chorizo. In a 4-qt. Dutch oven cook chorizo and garlic until chorizo is browned; drain off fat.

2. Stir next five ingredients (through cumin) into Dutch oven. Bring to boiling; reduce heat. Simmer, covered, 15 minutes. Stir in pasta, zucchini, and corn. Simmer, uncovered, 5 minutes more or until pasta is tender but still firm, stirring occasionally. If desired, stir in cilantro.

FOR 12 SERVINGS Use a 6- to 8-qt. Dutch oven.

PER SERVING *481 cal., 30 g fat (11 g sat. fat), 67 mg chol., 1,875 mg sodium, 28 g carb., 1 g fiber, 23 g pro.*

Italian Sausage and Two-Bean Skillet

Cannellini beans are fairly widely available, but if you can't find them, you can use Great Northern beans or navy beans instead. Both are smaller than cannellini beans.

1. In an extra-large skillet heat oil over medium heat. Add sausage and cook 10 minutes, turning occasionally. Add shallots and garlic; cook 30 seconds. Add chicken broth and bring to boiling; reduce heat. Simmer, covered, 5 minutes.

2. Add green beans and cannellini beans to skillet; return to simmer. Cover and cook 5 minutes more or until green beans are crisp-tender and sausage is done (160°F). Add tomatoes and parsley to skillet; stir to combine.

*TIP Four uncooked sausage links is about 1 lb.; eight uncooked sausage links is about 2 lb.

PER SERVING *573 cal., 40 g fat (13 g sat. fat), 86 mg chol., 1,345 mg sodium, 28 g carb., 8 g fiber, 26 g pro.*

START TO FINISH 25 minutes

4 servings	ingredients	8 servings
1 Tbsp.	olive oil	2 Tbsp.
4	uncooked Italian sausage links*	8
½ cup	sliced shallots, peeled and sliced	1 cup
1 Tbsp.	minced garlic	2 Tbsp.
2 cups	reduced-sodium chicken broth	4 cups
12 oz.	green beans, trimmed	1½ lb.
one 15- to 16-oz. can	cannellini beans, rinsed and drained	two 15- to 16-oz. cans
1¾ cups	cherry tomatoes, halved	3½ cups
⅓ cup	chopped Italian parsley	⅔ cup

Two-Cheese Beer Soup

This is not diet food, but boy, is it good. As if the two cheeses weren't tantalizing enough, it also calls for sausage and hash brown potatoes. It will warm you up, from the inside out, on the coldest night.

1. Allow sharp and white cheddar cheeses to stand at room temperature 30 minutes. Meanwhile, in a 4-qt. pot or Dutch oven melt butter over medium heat. Add kielbasa and onion and cook until onion is tender and sausage is browned, stirring occasionally.

2. Stir in flour, mustard, and thyme (mixture will be thick). Add broth all at once. Cook and stir until bubbly. Add beer and potatoes. Bring to boiling; reduce heat. Simmer, uncovered, 5 minutes, stirring occasionally. Add cream and heat through.

3. Gradually add cheeses, stirring after each addition until melted. Stir in green onions. Serve with additional shredded cheese, additional chopped green onions, and/or hot sauce.

FOR 12 SERVINGS Use a 6- to 8-qt. pot or Dutch oven.

PER SERVING *639 cal., 50 g fat (27 g sat. fat), 140 mg chol., 1,102 mg sodium, 23 g carb., 2 g fiber, 23 g pro.*

START TO FINISH 45 minutes

6 servings	ingredients	12 servings
1½ cups	shredded sharp cheddar cheese	3 cups
1¼ cups	white cheddar cheese, shredded	2½ cups
3 Tbsp.	butter	6 Tbsp.
8 to 10 oz.	cooked kielbasa, sliced	16 to 20 oz.
½ cup	finely chopped onion	1 cup
⅓ cup	all-purpose flour	⅔ cup
½ tsp.	dry mustard	1 tsp.
½ tsp.	dried thyme or oregano, crushed	1 tsp.
two 14.5-oz. cans	reduced-sodium chicken broth	four 14.5-oz. cans
one 12-oz. bottle	ale beer	two 12-oz. bottles
2 cups	frozen diced hash brown potatoes	4 cups
1 cup	heavy cream	2 cups
½ cup	chopped green onions	1 cup
	Bottled hot pepper sauce	

CHAPTER 4

Seafood

Dishes featuring fish and shellfish are naturally elegant—perfect for entertaining, whether it's simple fillets baked in wine or New Orleans-style shrimp.

112

116

130

Tuna with Grilled Cherry Vinaigrette and Couscous

Although it's possible to pit a cherry with a clean paper clip (pull off the stem, insert the paper clip, and twist it around to loosen the pit and pull it out), the easiest way to pit cherries is with a tool made for that purpose. Cherry pitters are inexpensive and available at kitchen stores and online.

PREP 40 minutes
MARINATE 30 minutes   **GRILL** 8 minutes

4 servings	ingredients	8 servings
four 6-oz.	fresh or frozen tuna steaks, 1 inch thick	eight 6-oz.
3 cups	fresh sweet cherries, pitted	6 cups
¼ cup	red wine vinegar	½ cup
2 Tbsp.	honey	¼ cup
1 Tbsp.	finely chopped shallot	2 Tbsp.
1 Tbsp.	Dijon mustard	2 Tbsp.
½ tsp.	snipped fresh thyme	1 tsp.
¼ tsp.	salt	½ tsp.
⅛ to ¼ tsp.	cayenne pepper	¼ to ½ tsp.
¼ cup	olive oil	½ cup
1½ cups	chicken broth	3 cups
1 cup	couscous	2 cups
1 cup	shredded fresh spinach leaves	2 cups
¼ cup	chopped toasted hazelnuts*	½ cup
2 oz.	ricotta salata, crumbled, or Brie cheese, cubed	4 oz.

1. If using wooden skewers, soak in water 30 minutes. Thaw tuna, if frozen.

2. Meanwhile, thread cherries onto skewers. Grill cherries, covered, over medium heat 5 minutes or until lightly charred, turning once. Remove cherries from skewers. Halve half the cherries; set aside.

3. For marinade, in a blender or food processor combine remaining cherries and next seven ingredients (through cayenne pepper). Cover and blend or process until smooth. With blender or processor running, slowly add oil in a steady stream until thickened. Reserve half the marinade; cover and chill until needed.

4. Rinse tuna; pat dry with paper towels. Place tuna in a resealable plastic bag set in a shallow dish. Pour remaining marinade over tuna. Seal bag; turn to coat tuna. Marinate in the refrigerator 30 to 60 minutes.

5. In a medium saucepan bring broth to boiling. Stir in couscous; remove from heat. Cover and let stand 5 minutes. Fluff with a fork. Stir in reserved cherries, spinach, and hazelnuts.

6. Drain tuna, reserving marinade. Grease grill rack. Grill tuna, covered, over medium heat 8 to 12 minutes or just until fish flakes, turning and brushing once with marinade.

7. Slice tuna. Drizzle reserved marinade over tuna and couscous and sprinkle with ricotta salata.

*TIP To toast hazelnuts, preheat oven to 350°F. Spread nuts in a single layer in a shallow baking pan. Bake 8 to 10 minutes or until light brown, stirring once to brown evenly. Cool slightly. Place the warm nuts on a clean kitchen towel; rub with the towel to remove the loose skins. Or refer to Tip, page 89.

PER SERVING *675 cal., 22 g fat (5 g sat. fat), 81 mg chol., 802 mg sodium, 66 g carb., 6 g fiber, 52 g pro.*

Muffin Pan Tuna Melts

Stuffed with tuna, dilled Havarti, shallot, dried cranberries, and honey mustard, this fun twist on the classic tuna melt is fancy enough for a company lunch. Add a soup or salad to round out the meal.

1. Preheat oven to 375°F. Generously coat twelve 2½-inch muffin cups with cooking spray. Lightly brush one side of bread slices with melted butter. Press bread slices, buttered sides up, into prepared muffin cups.

2. In a small bowl combine the next six ingredients (through honey mustard). Spoon 2 Tbsp. filling into each bread-lined muffin cup.

3. Bake 15 minutes or until filling is hot and bubbly. Remove tuna melts from muffin cups; let stand 5 minutes before serving. If desired, top with dill and/or hot peppers.

FOR 12 SERVINGS Use two twelve-cup muffin pans.

PER SERVING *268 cal., 14 g fat (6 g sat. fat), 46 mg chol., 516 mg sodium, 20 g carb., 2 g fiber, 18 g pro.*

PREP 25 minutes
BAKE 15 minutes **STAND** 5 minutes

6 servings	ingredients	12 servings
	Nonstick cooking spray	
12 slices	honey oat or honey wheat bread, crusts removed	24 slices
2 Tbsp.	light butter with canola oil, melted	¼ cup
two 5-oz. cans	chunk white tuna (water pack), drained	four 5-oz. cans
4 oz.	Havarti cheese with dill, cut into small cubes	8 oz.
3 Tbsp.	light mayonnaise	¼ cup + 2 Tbsp.
2 Tbsp.	snipped dried cranberries	¼ cup
2 Tbsp.	finely chopped shallot	¼ cup
1 Tbsp.	honey mustard	2 Tbsp.
	Fresh dill sprigs (optional)	
	Pickled hot peppers (optional)	

Tuscan Tuna Salad

Albacore tuna is the meatiest, densest, and whitest of all of the types of tuna. It comes packed in both water and oil. You'll need the type packed in oil for this recipe, as the oil helps to dress the salad.

1. Remove 1 tsp. zest and juice lemon.

2. In a large bowl combine beans, tuna, and onion. Add lemon zest, lemon juice, arugula, and tomatoes; toss to combine. Season to taste with salt and pepper.

FOR 8 SERVINGS In Step 1, remove 2 tsp. lemon zest.

PER SERVING *181 cal., 4 g fat (1 g sat. fat), 31 mg chol., 544 mg sodium, 19 g carb., 6 g fiber, 22 g pro.*

START TO FINISH 10 minutes

4 servings	ingredients	8 servings
1	lemon	2
one 15-oz. can	cannellini beans (white kidney beans), rinsed and drained	two 15-oz. cans
two 5-oz. cans	albacore tuna packed in oil, undrained and broken into chunks	four 5-oz. cans
½ cup	thinly sliced red onion	1 cup
4 cups	lightly packed arugula or mixed spring greens	8 cups
1 cup	grape or cherry tomatoes, halved	2 cups
	Salt	
	Black pepper	

Pacific Salmon Chowder

If you can't find skinless salmon fillets, buy fresh and ask at the meat counter to have the skin removed.

1. Thaw salmon, if frozen. Rinse salmon; pat dry with paper towels. Cut into 1-inch pieces.

2. In a 4-qt. pot melt butter over medium heat. Add chopped fennel; cook 5 to 6 minutes or until tender, stirring occasionally. Add garlic; cook and stir 1 minute more.

3. Add the next four ingredients (through pepper). Bring to boiling; reduce heat. Simmer, uncovered, 10 minutes or until potatoes are tender.

4. In a bowl combine 1 cup of the half-and-half and the flour; stir into soup. Cook and stir until slightly thickened and bubbly. Stir in salmon. Return just to boiling; reduce heat. Simmer gently, uncovered, 3 to 5 minutes or until salmon flakes easily. Stir in remaining half-and-half; heat through. Stir in lemon zest. Top servings with fennel fronds.

FOR 12 SERVINGS In Step 4, use 2 cups of the half-and-half.

PER SERVING *286 cal., 14 g fat (6 g sat. fat), 69 mg chol., 651 mg sodium, 20 g carb., 2 g fiber, 21 g pro.*

PREP 20 minutes
COOK 30 minutes

6 servings	ingredients	12 servings
1 lb.	fresh or frozen skinless salmon fillets	2 lb.
1 Tbsp.	butter	2 Tbsp.
½ cup	chopped fennel (reserve fronds)	1 cup
2	cloves garlic, minced	4
one 32-oz. box	reduced-sodium chicken or vegetable broth	two 32-oz. boxes
1¼ lb.	Yukon gold potatoes, peeled (if desired) and cut into ½-inch pieces	2½ lb.
½ tsp.	salt	1 tsp.
¼ tsp.	black pepper	½ tsp.
1½ cups	half-and-half	3 cups
2 Tbsp.	all-purpose flour	¼ cup
1 tsp.	lemon zest	2 tsp.

Fish and Tomatoes in Wine

Poaching the fish in a combination of dry white wine, water, and olive oil infuses it with flavor and keeps it super moist and delicately textured—not to mention it smells heavenly as it cooks!

1. In a large skillet combine wine, water, and oil. Add tomatoes, shallots, thyme, and salt. Bring to boiling; reduce heat. Simmer 3 to 5 minutes or until tomatoes are softened.

2. Place fish in skillet, spooning some of the wine mixture over fish. Cook, covered, over medium-low heat 8 to 10 minutes or until fish flakes easily. Remove and discard thyme.

3. Using a slotted spoon, transfer fish and tomatoes to shallow bowls, breaking fish into chunks. Ladle wine mixture over fish. Top with additional fresh thyme.

PER SERVING *272 cal., 16 g fat (2 g sat. fat), 91 mg chol., 155 mg sodium, 5 g carb., 1 g fiber, 21 g pro.*

START TO FINISH 25 minutes

4 servings	ingredients	8 servings
½ cup	dry white wine	1 cup
¼ cup	water	½ cup
¼ cup	olive oil	½ cup
2 cups	cherry or grape tomatoes	4 cups
2	shallots, sliced ¼ inch thick	4
6	fresh thyme sprigs	12
¼ tsp.	kosher salt	½ tsp.
1 lb.	fresh skinless halibut, striped bass, or red snapper fillets, cut into 4 portions	2 lb.

Fish and Veggies en Papillote

"En papillote" is French for "in parchment," and refers to a technique of cooking foods—especially delicate foods such as fish and vegetables—enclosed in a pouch. It helps keep the fish moist and allows the ingredients to mingle. It also makes a very pretty presentation!

1. Preheat oven to 375°F. For each packet, lay out one piece of parchment on a flat surface, one side toward you. Place a piece of fish in the center. Season with some of the salt and black pepper. Stack a few pieces of each vegetable on the fish. Drizzle with some of the oil and top with garlic. Season with more salt and pepper. Starting from the side toward you, fold bottom edge of parchment up and over the fish. Fold in the ends of the parchment over the fish. Roll fish in packet over once. Fold the corners on the top edge in toward the center to form a point (like an envelope). Roll up, tucking in the pointed end on the folded edge of the pouch.

2. Arrange packets on a large baking sheet. Bake 20 to 25 minutes or until fish flakes easily. Carefully open pouches. Serve with additional oil and with lime wedges and mint.

PER SERVING *307 cal., 16 g fat (2 g sat. fat), 102 mg chol., 484 mg sodium, 7 g carb., 2 g fiber, 34 g pro.*

PREP 30 minutes
BAKE 20 minutes

6 servings	ingredients	12 servings
6	12×15-inch squares parchment paper	12
six 6-oz.	1-inch thick skinless white fish fillets, such as sea bass, halibut, or cod	twelve 6-oz.
1 tsp.	kosher salt	2 tsp.
½ tsp.	freshly ground black pepper	1 tsp.
½	large red sweet pepper, cut into bite-size strips	1
½	large yellow sweet pepper, cut into bite-size strips	1
½	Anaheim chile pepper, stemmed and sliced (tip, page 15)	1
half 9-oz. bunch	Broccolini, trimmed	one 9 oz. bunch
½	small red onion, sliced	1
5½ Tbsp.	extra-virgin olive oil	⅔ cup + 1 Tbsp.
6	cloves garlic, sliced	12
	Extra-virgin olive oil	
	Lime wedges	
	Fresh mint	

Oven-Fried Fish Torta with Mexican Cocktail Sauce

The pickled red onions are the "wow" factor on this multidimensional sandwich. They're charred before being soaked in a brine of grapefruit, orange, and lime juices; salt; oregano; garlic; and cracked black pepper. They add lively flavor to the crisp crusted fish slathered with spicy cocktail sauce.

1. For the pickled onions, preheat broiler. Line a 15×10-inch baking pan with foil. Arrange onion slices in prepared pan. Broil 4 to 5 inches from heat 14 minutes or until charred, turning once. Cool slightly. Separate into rings, discarding any dry blackened pieces. If desired, coarsely chop onion. In a medium bowl combine the charred onion and the next seven ingredients (through cracked black pepper). Cover and chill 2 to 24 hours.

2. Thaw fish, if frozen. Preheat oven to 425°F. Line a baking sheet with foil. For sauce, in a small bowl combine cocktail sauce, cilantro, lime juice, jalapeño, and cumin.

3. Rinse fish; pat dry. In a shallow dish stir together cornflakes, garlic powder, chili powder, and cayenne pepper. In a second shallow dish beat egg with a fork. Coat fish with flour and sprinkle with salt. Dip fish into egg, then into corn flake mixture, pressing lightly to adhere. Place fish on prepared baking sheet. Bake 10 to 12 minutes or until fish flakes easily.

4. Spread rolls with sauce and fill with lettuce, fish, and pickled onions. Cut sandwiches in half.

PER SERVING *497 cal., 8 g fat (2 g sat. fat), 103 mg chol., 1,153 mg sodium, 70 g carb., 5 g fiber, 35 g pro.*

PREP 20 minutes **BROIL** 14 minutes **BAKE** 10 minutes **CHILL** 2 hours

4 servings	ingredients	8 servings
1	large red onion, cut into ½-inch slices	2
¼ cup	grapefruit juice	½ cup
2 Tbsp.	orange juice	¼ cup
2 Tbsp.	lime juice	¼ cup
1 tsp.	kosher salt	2 tsp.
1 tsp.	dried oregano	2 tsp.
1	clove garlic, minced	2
¼ tsp.	cracked black pepper	½ tsp.
two 8-oz.	fresh or frozen skinless tilapia fillets, about ½ inch thick	four 8-oz.
¼ cup	cocktail sauce	½ cup
1½ tsp.	snipped fresh cilantro	1 Tbsp.
1½ tsp.	lime juice	1 Tbsp.
¼ to ½	jalapeño-seeded and finely chopped (tip, page 15)	½ to 1
¼ tsp.	ground cumin	½ tsp.
¾ cup	corn flakes, crushed	1½ cups
1 tsp.	garlic powder	2 tsp.
1 tsp.	chili powder	2 tsp.
⅛ to ¼ tsp.	cayenne pepper	¼ to ½ tsp.
1	egg	2
1 Tbsp.	all-purpose flour	2 Tbsp.
	Salt	
two 8-inch	Mexican bolillos or hard rolls, split and toasted	four 8-inch
	Shredded lettuce	

Crusty Fish Sticks

The key to the crunch on these fish sticks is preheating a cast-iron skillet in the oven and then adding the oil and fish before returning to the oven to bake. The contact with the hot surface of the pan immediately creates a crisp crust.

PREP 30 minutes   BAKE 18 minutes
CHILL 20 minutes   STAND 5 minutes

4 servings	ingredients	8 servings
1	lemon	2
½ cup	mayonnaise	1 cup
¼ cup	finely chopped fresh cilantro	½ cup
1	cloves garlic, minced	2
⅛ tsp.	cayenne pepper	¼ tsp.
1 tsp.	salt	2 tsp.
12 oz.	haddock or cod fillets, cut into 3×¾-inch sticks	1½ lb.
¼ tsp.	black pepper	½ tsp.
½ cup	buttermilk	1 cup
2 tsp.	bottled hot pepper sauce	4 tsp.
¾ cup	cornstarch	1½ cups
⅛ tsp.	black pepper	¼ tsp.
2	eggs	4
1 cup	panko bread crumbs	2 cups
2 tsp.	dried cilantro or parsley	4 tsp.
½ tsp.	garlic powder	1 tsp.
½ cup	olive oil	1 cup
	Fresh cilantro (optional)	

1. Place a 12-inch cast-iron skillet in the oven. Preheat oven to 425°F. Remove 2 tsp. zest and 1 tsp. juice from lemon. For aïoli, in a bowl whisk together mayonnaise, fresh cilantro, lemon juice, garlic, cayenne, and ⅛ tsp. of the salt. Cover and chill until serving.

2. Season fish with ¼ tsp. of the salt and ¼ tsp. black pepper. Place in a large resealable plastic bag. In a bowl whisk together the buttermilk and hot pepper sauce; pour over fish. Seal bag; set in a bowl. Chill 20 minutes.

3. Place cornstarch in a shallow dish; add ⅛ tsp. salt and ⅛ tsp. black pepper. In a second shallow dish lightly beat the eggs. In a third shallow dish combine the lemon zest, panko, dried cilantro, garlic powder, and remaining salt.

4. Drain fish, discarding any remaining marinade. Gently dip fish in cornstarch to coat, then dip in eggs to moisten. Dip in panko mixture to coat. Transfer to a baking sheet.

5. Carefully remove skillet from oven; add olive oil. Carefully arrange fish sticks in skillet. Bake 10 minutes or until browned on the bottom. Turn and bake 8 to 10 minutes more or until golden and fish flakes easily. Drain on paper towels 5 minutes. Drizzle with additional lemon juice; serve with aïoli. Top with fresh cilantro, if desired.

FOR 8 SERVINGS In Step 1, remove 4 tsp. zest and 2 tsp. juice from lemons. Use ¼ tsp. salt. In Step 2, use ½ tsp. each salt and black pepper. In Step 3, add ¼ tsp. each salt and black pepper to the cornstarch.

PER SERVING *570 cal., 44 g fat (7 g sat. fat), 151 mg chol., 895 mg sodium, 23 g carb., 1 g fiber, 19 g pro.*

Open-Face Flounder Sandwich

If you can find herb salad mix in your supermarket, it would be a shortcut to mixing up the herbs and greens for the topping on this sandwich.

1. Squeeze juice from half the lemon; cut remaining half into wedges. For sauce, in a small bowl combine lemon juice, mayonnaise, shallot, relish, and mustard. Season to taste with pepper.

2. Rinse fish; pat dry with paper towels. Cut fish into four portions; sprinkle lightly with salt. Sprinkle flour onto a plate. Dip fish into flour, turning to coat. In a large skillet heat oil over medium-high heat. Add fish, in batches if needed. Cook 4 to 6 minutes per ½-inch thickness or until fish flakes easily with a fork, turning once.

3. Spread bread slices with sauce and sprinkle with half the herbs and greens. Top with fish and remaining herbs and greens. Serve with lemon wedges.

FOR 8 SERVINGS In Step 2, cut fish into eight portions.

PER SERVING *555 cal., 29 g fat (4 g sat. fat), 89 mg chol., 841 mg sodium, 39 g carb., 4 g fiber, 37 g pro.*

START TO FINISH 30 minutes

4 servings	ingredients	8 servings
1	lemon, halved	2
⅓ cup	mayonnaise	⅔ cup
2 Tbsp.	finely chopped shallot	¼ cup
1 Tbsp.	pickle relish	2 Tbsp.
1 tsp.	Dijon mustard	2 tsp.
	Freshly ground black pepper	
1½ lb.	fresh flounder or other firm white fish fillets	3 lb.
	Kosher salt	
2 Tbsp.	all-purpose flour	¼ cup
3 Tbsp.	vegetable oil	¼ cup + 2 Tbsp.
4 slices	sourdough bread, toasted	8 slices
4 cups	mixed herbs and greens, such as parsley, chives, basil, cilantro, spinach, and/or sorrel, coarsely chopped	8 cups

Cod and Tomatoes with Crispy Parsley Crumbs

Cod is often paired with tomatoes—the acidity in the tomatoes complements the rich, buttery-texture fish. This dish is simple but elegant enough for a nice dinner party. Serve with steamed buttered green beans tossed with toasted almonds.

1. Preheat oven to 425°F. Coat a shallow baking pan with nonstick cooking spray. In a small bowl combine panko, parsley, shallot, butter, and half the salt and pepper.

2. Arrange fish in baking pan. Sprinkle with remaining salt and pepper. Top with half the crumb mixture. Squeeze seeds from tomato halves around fish. Place tomatoes around fish, cut sides up. Top with remaining crumb mixture. Bake 20 minutes or until fish flakes easily with a fork and crumbs are golden.

PER SERVING *287 cal., 12 g fat (7 g sat. fat), 96 mg chol., 434 mg sodium, 17 g carb., 3 g fiber, 28 g pro.*

PREP 20 minutes
BAKE 20 minutes

4 servings	ingredients	8 servings
	Nonstick cooking spray	
¾ cup	panko bread crumbs	1½ cups
½ cup	finely chopped fresh Italian parsley leaves	1 cup
½ cup	finely chopped shallot	1 cup
¼ cup	butter, melted	½ cup
½ tsp.	salt	1 tsp.
½ tsp.	black pepper	1 tsp.
4	cod fillets, 1 inch thick	8
6	small tomatoes, halved crosswise	12

Weeknight Paella

Saffron is the stamens of a crocus flower that are harvested by hand—which is why it's the most expensive spice in the world. Paella wouldn't be paella without the distinctive flavor and sunny yellow color it imparts though—and thankfully a little goes a long way.

1. Thaw scallops and shrimp, if frozen. Rinse scallops; pat dry. Cut any large scallops in half. Prepare rice according to microwave package directions. Stir in turmeric.

2. Meanwhile, in an extra-large skillet heat oil over medium-high heat. Add scallops; cook 2 minutes or until opaque, turning once. Remove from skillet. Reduce heat to medium and add sausage to skillet. Cook and stir 2 to 4 minutes or until heated through and starting to brown. Stir in tomatoes and saffron. Cook and stir 2 minutes more.

3. Stir hot rice, shrimp, and scallops into sausage mixture. Heat through. Season to taste with salt and pepper. If desired, sprinkle with parsley.

PER SERVING *537 cal., 25 g fat (7 g sat. fat), 160 mg chol., 1,360 mg sodium, 40 g carb., 3 g fiber, 38 g pro.*

START TO FINISH 25 minutes

4 servings	ingredients	8 servings
8 oz.	fresh or frozen sea scallops	16 oz.
8 oz.	fresh or frozen peeled and deveined cooked shrimp	16 oz.
two 10-oz. pkg.	frozen long grain white rice with peas, corn, and carrots	four 10-oz. pkg.
2 tsp.	ground turmeric	4 tsp.
1 Tbsp.	canola oil	2 Tbsp.
8 oz.	cooked, smoked chorizo sausage links, halved and sliced	1 lb.
1⅓ cups	coarsely chopped roma tomatoes	2⅔ cups
¼ tsp.	saffron threads, crushed	½ tsp.
	Salt and black pepper	
	Snipped fresh Italian parsley (optional)	

Drunken Shrimp and Scallop Kabobs

The base of the marinade for this shellfish dish approximates a less-sweet margarita—tequila, lime, and just a hint of sugar, plus olive oil, garlic, oregano, and paprika.

1. If using wooden skewers, soak in water 30 minutes. Thaw scallops and shrimp, if frozen. Peel and devein shrimp, leaving tails intact if desired. Rinse scallops and shrimp; pat dry. Place in a resealable plastic bag set in a shallow dish.

2. For marinade, in a small bowl combine next eight ingredients (through paprika). Remove ½ cup marinade for jicama slaw. Pour remaining marinade over scallops and shrimp. Seal bag; turn to coat. Marinate at room temperature 15 minutes, turning bag once or twice.

3. Meanwhile, for jicama slaw, in a medium bowl combine jicama, avocado, and cilantro. Pour reserved marinade over slaw; toss gently to coat. Season to taste with pepper and additional salt. Cover and chill until ready to serve.

4. Drain scallops and shrimp, discarding marinade. Alternately thread scallops and shrimp onto six long skewers, leaving ¼ inch between pieces. Grill kabobs, covered, over medium-high heat 8 to 10 minutes or until scallops and shrimp are opaque, turning once. Serve with jicama slaw and lime wedges.

FOR 12 SERVINGS In Step 2, reserve 1 cup marinade for the slaw.

PER SERVING *261 cal., 9 g fat (1 g sat. fat), 103 mg chol., 1,323 mg sodium, 17 g carb., 6 g fiber, 25 g pro.*

PREP 25 minutes
MARINATE 15 minutes **GRILL** 8 minutes

6 servings	ingredients	12 servings
1¾ lb.	fresh or frozen large sea scallops	3½ lb.
12 oz.	fresh or frozen large shrimp in shells	24 oz.
¼ cup	tequila	½ cup
¼ cup	lime juice	½ cup
¼ cup	olive oil	½ cup
2 Tbsp.	snipped fresh oregano	¼ cup
4	cloves garlic, sliced	8
2 tsp.	sugar	4 tsp.
2 tsp.	salt	4 tsp.
½ tsp.	paprika	1 tsp.
4 cups	thin bite-size strips jicama	8 cups
1	avocado, halved, seeded, peeled, and thinly sliced	2
½ cup	fresh cilantro leaves	1 cup
	Black pepper	
	Lime wedges	

Lemony Shrimp and Orzo

PREP 30 minutes
BAKE 15 minutes   STAND 5 minutes

4 servings	ingredients	8 servings
½ lb.	large fresh or frozen shrimp	1 lb.
½ lb.	red Swiss chard, stems removed	1 lb.
2	small lemons	4
1 Tbsp.	unsalted butter	2 Tbsp.
1 Tbsp.	minced shallot	2 Tbsp.
1 Tbsp.	all-purpose flour	2 Tbsp.
2¾ cups	chicken stock or reduced-sodium chicken broth	5½ cups
¼ tsp.	salt	½ tsp.
⅛ tsp.	black pepper	¼ tsp.
1 Tbsp.	snipped fresh dill weed	2 Tbsp.
8 oz.	dried orzo pasta	1 lb.
½ cup	crumbled feta cheese	1 cup

Swiss chard adds fresh, earthy flavor—and lots of nutrients—to this one-dish meal. If you like, substitute kale or spinach for the chard.

1. Preheat oven to 400°F. Butter an 8-inch or 9-inch baking pan; set aside. Thaw shrimp, if frozen. Peel and devein shrimp; set aside. In a 3-qt. pot combine chard and ¼ cup water. Bring to boiling; reduce heat. Cook, covered, 5 minutes or until tender, stirring occasionally. Drain, pressing to remove liquid. Coarsely chop chard.

2. Remove 1½ tsp. zest and 2 Tbsp. juice from one lemon; thinly slice remaining lemon. In same pot melt butter over medium heat. Add shallot; cook 1 minute. Add flour; cook 1 minute. Add chicken stock, salt, and pepper. Bring to boiling; reduce heat. Simmer, uncovered, 5 minutes or until slightly thickened. Stir in lemon zest, juice, and dill.

3. Place uncooked orzo in prepared dish. Top with cooked chard and feta. Top with shrimp. Sprinkle with additional salt and black pepper. Pour broth mixture over shrimp; stir lightly. Top with lemon slices. Bake, covered, 15 to 18 minutes or until pasta is tender and shrimp are opaque. Let stand 5 minutes before serving (mixture will thicken as it stands). Top with additional fresh dill weed.

FOR 8 SERVINGS In Step 1, use a 13×9-inch baking dish, 4- to 5-qt. pot, and ½ cup water. In Step 2, remove 1 Tbsp. zest and ¼ cup juice from two lemons and thinly slice remaining lemons.

PER SERVING *361 cal., 8 g fat (5 g sat. fat), 104 mg chol., 858 mg sodium, 50 g carb., 4 g fiber, 23 g pro.*

Shrimp New Orleans

Put on some old-school jazz while you cook and you'll be transported to the Big Easy without setting foot outside your kitchen.

PREP 30 minutes
BAKE 30 minutes

6 servings	ingredients	12 servings
12 oz.	fresh or frozen, peeled and deveined cooked shrimp	1½ lb.
2 Tbsp.	butter	4 Tbsp.
½ cup	chopped onion	1 cup
¼ cup	chopped green or red sweet pepper	½ cup
2 cups	cooked white rice	4 cups
one 10.75-oz. can	condensed cream of shrimp soup	two 10.75 oz. cans
½ cup	half-and-half	1 cup
2 Tbsp.	dry sherry	¼ cup
1 tsp.	lemon juice	2 tsp.
¼ tsp.	salt	½ tsp.
⅛ tsp.	cayenne pepper	¼ tsp.
	Snipped fresh cilantro	

1. Thaw shrimp, if frozen. Preheat oven to 350°F. In a large saucepan melt butter over medium heat. Add onion and sweet pepper; cook until tender, stirring occasionally. Remove from heat.

2. Stir in the next seven ingredients (through cayenne pepper). Transfer to a 2-qt. baking dish.

3. Bake 30 minutes or until heated through. Sprinkle with cilantro and, if desired, additional cayenne.

FOR 12 SERVINGS In Step 2, use a 3-qt. baking dish.

PER SERVING *227 cal., 9 g fat (5 g sat. fat), 116 mg chol., 553 mg sodium, 21 g carb., 1 g fiber, 15 g pro.*

Buttery Poached Shrimp Salad

This pretty salad is packed with spring ingredients, including beets, baby potatoes, and butter lettuce. Serve with chilled white wine or iced tea.

1. Thaw shrimp, if frozen. Peel and devein shrimp, leaving tails intact if desired. Rinse shrimp; pat dry. Chill until needed. Remove 1 tsp. zest and squeeze 3 Tbsp. juice from lemon.

2. Preheat oven to 400°F. Line a baking sheet with foil. Arrange beet slices on prepared baking sheet. Brush with half the oil. Bake 20 to 25 minutes or until tender.

3. Meanwhile, in a Dutch oven cook potatoes in boiling, lightly salted water 15 minutes or until tender. Using a slotted spoon, remove potatoes.

4. Reduce heat to medium-low. Add shrimp to water in Dutch oven. Cook 2 to 3 minutes or until opaque. Drain shrimp in a colander. In same Dutch oven melt butter; stir in lemon zest and juice, remaining oil, chives, and pepper. Add potatoes and shrimp; toss to coat.

5. Line a platter with lettuce. Arrange beets, potatoes, and shrimp on lettuce. If desired, sprinkle with additional chives.

FOR 8 SERVINGS In Step 1, remove 2 tsp. zest and 6 Tbsp. juice from lemon.

PER SERVING *351 cal., 16 g fat (7 g sat. fat), 182 mg chol., 255 mg sodium, 30 g carb., 6 g fiber, 24 g pro.*

PREP 25 minutes
BAKE 20 minutes

4 servings	ingredients	8 servings
1 lb.	fresh or frozen large shrimp in shells	2 lb.
1	medium lemon	2
8 oz.	red and/or yellow beets, peeled and sliced ¼ inch thick	16 oz.
2 Tbsp.	olive oil	¼ cup
1¼ lb.	tiny yellow new potatoes, halved	2½ lb.
3 Tbsp.	butter	6 Tbsp.
2 Tbsp.	chopped fresh chives	¼ cup
½ tsp.	cracked black pepper	1 tsp.
1	head butterhead bibb, lettuce torn into small pieces	2

Warm Shrimp and Baby Dutch Potato Salad

Here's a quick way to trim fresh green beans: Line up a handful of beans at a time on a cutting board with the stem ends facing the same direction. One quick slice with a knife and they're ready to go.

1. In a 4- to 5-qt. Dutch oven cook potatoes in a large amount of boiling water 10 minutes. Add beans; return to boiling. Cook 4 minutes more or until potatoes are tender; drain

2. Meanwhile, in an extra-large bowl whisk together next five ingredients (through pepper). Gradually whisk in oil until combined. Add vegetables and shrimp; toss to coat. In a medium bowl toss greens with half the dill.

3. Serve warm potatoes over greens; sprinkle with remaining dill.

TIP If you prefer a chilled salad, cook and drain the potatoes and beans as directed, except rinse with cold water and drain again.

PER SERVING *326 cal., 14 g fat (2 g sat. fat), 183 mg chol., 621 mg sodium, 23 g carb., 5 g fiber, 26 g pro.*

START TO FINISH 30 minutes

4 servings	ingredients	8 servings
1 lb.	baby Dutch yellow potatoes	2 lb.
6 oz.	fresh green beans	12 oz.
¼ cup	cider vinegar	½ cup
1 Tbsp.	Dijon mustard	2 Tbsp.
2	cloves garlic, minced	4
½ tsp.	salt	1 tsp.
½ tsp.	black pepper	1 tsp.
¼ cup	olive oil	½ cup
1 lb.	frozen peeled and deveined cooked large shrimp, thawed	2 lb.
4 cups	mixed spring greens	8 cups
½ cup	fresh dill	1 cup

Shrimp Salad with Lime Dressing

For perfectly ripe, unblemished avocados, buy them when they're still firm and let them sit on the counter a day or two until the flesh barely gives when pressed with your finger. Transporting them from the store when they're still firm helps keep them from bumping around and getting bruised.

START TO FINISH 25 minutes

4 servings	ingredients	8 servings
1 large	lime	2 large
½ tsp.	kosher salt	1 tsp.
¼ tsp.	cayenne pepper	½ tsp.
2 Tbsp.	olive oil	¼ cup
1 lb.	fresh large shrimp in shells	2 lb.
1 tsp.	olive oil	2 tsp.
2	avocados, halved, seeded, peeled, and sliced	4
1 large	tomato, cut into chunks	2 large
1 cup	thinly sliced sweet onion	2 cups
½ cup	packed fresh cilantro	1 cup

1. If using wooden skewers, soak in water 30 minutes. For dressing, remove 1 tsp. zest and 3 Tbsp. juice from lime. In a small bowl combine lime zest and juice, half the salt, and cayenne pepper. Slowly whisk in 2 Tbsp. oil until combined.

2. Peel and devein shrimp, leaving tails intact if desired. Rinse shrimp; pat dry. In a medium bowl combine shrimp, 1 tsp. oil, and remaining salt; toss to coat. Thread shrimp onto skewers, leaving ¼ inch between shrimp. Grease grill rack. Grill shrimp kabobs, covered, over medium heat 3 to 4 minutes or until shrimp are opaque, turning once.

3. On a large platter arrange shrimp, avocados, tomato, and onion. Drizzle with dressing and sprinkle with cilantro.

FOR 8 SERVINGS In Step 1, remove 2 tsp. zest and 6 Tbsp. juice from limes. Use ¼ cup oil. In Step 2, use 2 tsp. oil.

PER SERVING *291 cal., 19 g fat (3 g sat. fat), 159 mg chol., 373 mg sodium, 12 g carb., 6 g fiber, 22 g pro.*

CHAPTER 5

Sides

Although the entrée seems to get more attention and thought, an extra-special side—a salad, veggie dish, and/or bread—can really make the meal.

136

147

159

Cheesy Baked Gnocchi with Kale

There's a lot going on in this dish—chewy gnocchi (potato dumplings), kale, and lots of cheese. Serve it with something simple, such as roast chicken.

1. Preheat oven to 400°F. Grease a 2-qt. baking dish; set aside. In a large pot cook gnocchi according to package directions, adding kale the last 1 minute. Drain; return pasta and kale to pot.

2. Meanwhile, in a saucepan cook garlic in butter over medium heat 1 minute. Stir in flour to combine. Whisk in milk; cook and stir until thickened and bubbly. Stir in Fontina and lemon zest. Pour over gnocchi mixture; stir to coat. Transfer to prepared baking dish. Top with Parmesan. Bake 20 minutes until lightly browned and bubbly. Sprinkle with black pepper, if desired.

FOR 16 SERVINGS In Step 1, use a 3 qt. baking dish.

PER SERVING *333 cal., 8 g fat (4 g sat. fat), 23 mg chol., 562 mg sodium, 53 g carb., 3 g fiber, 14 g pro.*

PREP 20 minutes
BAKE 20 minutes

8 servings	ingredients	16 servings
two 16-oz. pkg.	gnocchi	four 16-oz. pkg.
1 bunch	kale, washed, stemmed, and chopped	2 bunches
3	cloves garlic, minced	6
2 Tbsp.	butter	4 Tbsp.
2 Tbsp.	all-purpose flour	4 Tbsp.
1½ cups	milk	3 cups
½ cup	shredded Fontina or sharp white cheddar cheese	1 cup
1 Tbsp.	lemon zest	2 Tbsp.
½ cup	finely shredded Parmesan cheese	1 cup
	Black pepper (optional)	

Braised Brussels Sprouts with Crispy Shallots

Brussels sprouts have gained many new admirers the last few years, mostly because they're being cooked in ways other than being boiled until mushy. Here, they're braised in wine and broth and topped with strips of sweet, crispy shallots that taste like french-fried onions (or even better!).

START TO FINISH 40 minutes

6 servings	ingredients	12 servings
2 lb.	Brussels sprouts	4 lb.
3 Tbsp.	butter	6 Tbsp.
1 tsp.	kosher salt	2 tsp.
½ tsp.	dry mustard	1 tsp.
¼ cup	dry white wine	½ cup
½ cup	vegetable broth or mushroom broth	1 cup
2 Tbsp.	olive oil	¼ cup
1 cup	thinly sliced shallots	2 cups
¼ cup	cider vinegar	½ cup
	Black pepper	

1. Trim Brussels sprouts. In an extra-large skillet heat butter over medium-high heat. Add Brussels sprouts; toss to coat. Sprinkle with salt and dry mustard. Cook and stir 3 to 5 minutes or until sprouts are light brown.

2. Carefully add wine to skillet, stirring to scrape up any crusty brown bits. Add broth. Reduce heat to medium-low. Cook, covered, 8 to 10 minutes or just until sprouts are tender, stirring occasionally.

3. Meanwhile, in a large skillet heat oil over medium heat. Add shallots, breaking apart into individual rings. Cook 10 to 12 minutes or until deep brown and crisp, stirring frequently. Using tongs, transfer shallots to a paper towel-lined plate. Season to taste with additional salt.

4. Stir vinegar into sprouts. Increase heat to medium-high. Cook, uncovered, 2 minutes or until most of the liquid is evaporated. Remove from heat. Season to taste with additional salt and pepper. Serve topped with shallots.

PER SERVING *182 cal., 11 g fat (4 g sat. fat), 15 mg chol., 580 mg sodium, 17 g carb., 6 g fiber, 6 g pro.*

Honey-Cumin Roasted Carrots

This is the modern take on glazed carrots—and they're so much better than the cloyingly sweet dish you might have eaten growing up. Just a touch of honey is used in the glaze of sherry vinegar, garlic, cumin seeds, and olive oil. Try them with a beef roast and mashed potatoes.

1. Preheat oven to 375°F. In a baking pan toss together carrots, garlic cloves, cumin seeds, olive oil, sherry vinegar, and honey. Bake 30 to 35 minutes or until tender, stirring once.

PER SERVING *90 cal., 4 g fat (1 g sat. fat), 0 mg chol., 81 mg sodium, 13 g carb., 3 g fiber, 1 g pro.*

PREP 15 minutes
BAKE 45 minutes

4 servings	ingredients	8 servings
1 lb.	baby carrots with tops, trimmed and peeled, halved if large	2 lb.
2	cloves garlic, peeled	4
1 Tbsp.	cumin seeds	2 Tbsp.
1 Tbsp.	olive oil	2 Tbsp.
2 tsp.	sherry vinegar	4 tsp.
1 tsp.	honey	2 tsp.

Radish, Greens, and Bacon Sauté

Look for the freshest bunch of radishes you can find, as this dish calls for both the radish bottoms and green tops. The greens should be bright green, without any wilting or brown spots.

1. Remove, coarsely chop. and reserve radish tops. Quarter radishes.

2. In a skillet cook bacon over medium heat 4 minutes. Add radish quarters and onion to skillet in a single layer. Cook, stirring occasionally, 8 minutes or until bacon is crisp and radishes are light brown. Stir in radish tops and salt; cook 30 seconds more. Serve warm.

PER SERVING *98 cal., 8 g fat (3 g sat. fat), 13 mg chol., 305 mg sodium, 4 g carb., 2 g fiber, 3 g pro.*

START TO FINISH 25 minutes

4 servings	ingredients	8 servings
1 bunch	radishes with tops	2 bunches
2 slices	bacon, chopped	4 slices
1	small onion, halved and thinly sliced	2
¼ tsp.	salt	½ tsp.

Quinoa and Summer Vegetables

This all-in-one grain and vegetable side dish makes a nice accompaniment to grilled foods—especially lighter proteins such as salmon, shrimp, or chicken.

1. Cook quinoa according to package directions; transfer to a large bowl.

2. In a large skillet heat oil over medium-high heat. Add zucchini in a single layer. Cook, without stirring, 2 to 3 minutes or until browned on one side. Add a pinch of kosher salt. Stir; reduce heat to medium. Add sweet pepper; cook 2 minutes more, stirring occasionally, until crisp-tender. Stir in paprika; transfer to bowl with quinoa.

3. Stir in green onions, almonds, salt, and pepper. Stir in cilantro just before serving. Serve with lemon wedges.

PER SERVING *228 cal., 12 g fat (1 g sat. fat), 0 mg chol., 86 mg sodium, 26 g carb., 5 g fiber, 7 g pro.*

START TO FINISH 30 minutes

8 servings	ingredients	16 servings
1½ cups	quinoa, rinsed	3 cups
¼ cup	extra-virgin olive oil	½ cup
1	zucchini, chopped or sliced in ½-inch pieces	2
1	yellow, red, or orange sweet pepper, chopped	2
½ tsp.	smoked paprika	1 tsp.
6	green onions, bias-sliced	12
⅓ cup	almonds, toasted and coarsely chopped (tip, page 89)	⅔ cup
¼ tsp.	kosher salt	½ tsp.
¼ tsp.	freshly ground black pepper	½ tsp.
2 cups	loosely packed cilantro leaves	4 cups
	Lemon wedges	

Wild Rice Dressing

The nutty flavor of wild rice pairs perfectly with fall foods. This dish of wild and long-grain rice, veggies, toasted pine nuts, and Parmesan cheese is a natural alongside pork roast or chops.

1. Rinse uncooked wild rice in a strainer under cold water 1 minute; drain. In a large saucepan combine wild rice, broth, wine, uncooked brown rice (optional), and poultry seasoning. Bring to boiling; reduce heat. Simmer, covered, 40 minutes or until rice is tender. If using, add white rice the last 20 minutes of cooking time. If necessary, drain any remaining liquid.

2. Meanwhile, in a large skillet cook mushrooms, carrots, onions, and sweet pepper in hot butter over medium heat 5 to 8 minutes or until vegetables are tender. Stir in pine nuts, cheese, salt, and black pepper. Stir vegetables into rice.

FOR 12 SERVINGS In Step 2, use an extra-large skillet or Dutch oven.

PER SERVING *316 cal., 17 g fat (4 g sat. fat), 13 mg chol., 383 mg sodium, 30 g carb., 3 g fiber, 10 g pro.*

PREP 20 minutes
COOK 40 minutes

6 servings	ingredients	12 servings
½ cup	uncooked wild rice	1 cup
one 14.5-oz. can	reduced-sodium chicken broth	two 14.5-oz. cans
½ cup	dry white wine or chicken broth	1 cup
½ cup	uncooked white or brown rice (optional)	1 cup
½ tsp.	poultry seasoning	1 tsp.
2 cups	sliced fresh mushrooms, such as cremini, shiitake, and/or button	4 cups
1 cup	chopped carrots	2 cups
¾ cup	thinly sliced green onions	1½ cups
½ cup	chopped red sweet pepper	1 cup
2 Tbsp.	butter	4 Tbsp.
¾ cup	pine nuts, toasted (tip, page 8)	1½ cups
⅓ cup	finely shredded Parmesan cheese	⅔ cup
¼ tsp.	salt	½ tsp.
¼ tsp.	black pepper	½ tsp.

Mexican Diced Potato Hash

Queso Chihuahua is a soft, mild, white cheese that is good for melting. If you can't find it, Monterey Jack makes a fine substitute.

1. In a large heavy skillet heat oil over medium heat. Add potatoes; cook 18 minutes or until tender and brown, stirring occasionally. Add onion and salt; cook 4 minutes or until onion is tender.

2. Stir in tomato, jalapeño pepper, and cumin. Cook 3 minutes more or just until tomato is starting to soften and hash is heated through. If desired, sprinkle with cheese before serving.

FOR 8 SERVINGS In Step 1, use an extra-large heavy skillet or heavy Dutch oven.

PER SERVING *221 cal., 13 g fat (3 g sat. fat), 10 mg chol., 373 mg sodium, 22 g carb., 3 g fiber, 5 g pro.*

START TO FINISH 40 minutes

4 servings	ingredients	8 servings
3 Tbsp.	vegetable oil	¼ cup + 2 Tbsp.
1 lb.	round red potatoes, cut into ½-inch pieces	2 lb.
⅓ cup	chopped onion	⅔ cup
½ tsp.	salt	1 tsp.
1 cup	chopped tomato	2 cups
1	jalapeño or Anaheim chile pepper, seeded and chopped (tip, page 15)	2
1 tsp.	ground cumin	2 tsp.
⅓ cup	shredded queso Chihuahua or Monterey Jack cheese (optional)	⅔ cup

Roasted Smashed Potatoes

These little potato disks are crisp and cheesy on the outside and fluffy on the inside. Although they're lovely alongside a beef roast, you might want to make a tray of them just for snacking.

PREP 20 minutes   **COOK** 25 minutes
COOL 10 minutes   **ROAST** 22 minutes

6 servings	ingredients	12 servings
12 to 16	small red potatoes (1½ to 2 inches in diameter)	24 to 32
1¾ tsp.	salt	3½ tsp.
¼ cup	olive oil	½ cup
½ tsp.	black pepper	1 tsp.
¾ cup	finely shredded Parmesan cheese	1½ cups
2 Tbsp.	finely snipped fresh Italian parsley	¼ cup

1. In a large covered saucepan cook potatoes with 1 tsp. of the salt in enough boiling water to cover 25 to 30 minutes or until very tender; drain.

2. Preheat oven to 450°F. Line a 15×10-inch baking pan with foil. Transfer potatoes to prepared pan; cool 10 minutes. Using a potato masher or the palm of your hand, lightly press each potato to smash to ½-inch thickness, keeping potato in one piece. Brush with half the oil and sprinkle with ½ tsp. of the salt and half the pepper.

3. Roast 10 to 15 minutes or until bottoms are light brown and crisp. Turn potatoes; brush with remaining oil and sprinkle with remaining salt and pepper. Roast 10 to 15 minutes more or until potatoes are light brown and crisp.

4. In a small bowl combine cheese and parsley; sprinkle over potatoes. Roast 2 to 3 minutes or until cheese is melted.

FOR 12 SERVINGS In Step 1, use 2 tsp. salt.

PER SERVING *202 cal., 12 g fat (2 g sat. fat), 8 mg chol., 514 mg sodium, 18 g carb., 2 g fiber, 6 g pro.*

Cheesy Hasselback New Potatoes

Hasselback potatoes are a Swedish invention, named for the Stockholm restaurant at which they were first served. The buttered slices of potato separate as they roast, creating a crisp potato "fan" on top of a tender interior.

1. Slice into each new potato at ⅛-inch intervals, cutting to but not through opposite side. Arrange, cut sides up, on a greased baking pan. Brush with 2 Tbsp. of the butter. Cover with foil; bake at 400°F 45 minutes.

2. In a microwave-safe bowl heat semisoft cheese on 50 percent power 20 seconds. Place in a plastic bag; snip off one corner. In a small bowl combine bread crumbs, Parmesan, rosemary, and remaining melted butter.

3. Uncover potatoes; cool slightly. Using a butter knife, pry open layers; pipe cheese between. Sprinkle with bread crumb mixture. Bake 10 to 15 minutes more. Sprinkle with lemon zest.

FOR 12 SERVINGS In Step 1, use 4 Tbsp. melted butter.

PER SERVING *271 cal., 17 g fat (11 g sat. fat), 42 mg chol., 255 mg sodium, 26 g carb., 3 g fiber, 5 g pro.*

PREP 30 minutes
BAKE 55 minutes

6 servings	ingredients	12 servings
12	new potatoes	24
3 Tbsp.	butter, melted	6 Tbsp.
one 5.2-oz. pkg.	semisoft cheese with garlic and herbs	two 5.2-oz. pkg.
2 Tbsp.	fine dry bread crumbs	¼ cup
2 Tbsp.	grated Parmesan cheese	¼ cup
1 tsp.	chopped fresh rosemary	2 tsp.
2 tsp.	lemon zest	4 tsp.

Crisp Cornmeal Scones

Make these rich buttermilk scones in place of cornbread. They're equally good served with a bowl of spicy chili as they are alongside eggs at brunch.

1. Preheat oven to 425°F. In large bowl whisk together the first five ingredients (through salt).

2. Add shredded butter; toss to coat. (Or cut cubed butter into flour mixture with pastry blender until it resembles coarse crumbs). Make a well in center; add buttermilk. Stir until moistened; do not overmix. (If dough appears dry, add 1 to 2 tablespoons additional buttermilk.)

3. Turn dough out onto floured surface. Gently knead by lifting and folding dough, four or five times, giving a quarter turn after each knead. Pat into 8-inch square, ¾ inch thick. Cut into 2-inch squares. Place squares 1 inch apart on ungreased baking sheet. Brush with buttermilk; sprinkle with coarse sugar. Bake 12 to 15 minutes or until lightly browned; cool scones on a rack. Serve warm.

*TIP To shred butter, freeze butter 15 minutes. Use a coarse grater to shred butter. Toss into flour mixture or refrigerate, loosely covered, until needed.

**TIP For 1 cup sour milk, place 1 Tbsp. vinegar or lemon juice in a glass measure and enough milk to equal 1 cup. For 2 cups sour milk, use 2 Tbsp. vinegar or lemon juice and enough milk to equal 2 cups.

FOR 32 SERVINGS In Step 3, halve dough; pat into two 8-inch squares. Use two baking sheets.

PER SERVING *155 cal., 6 g fat (4 g sat. fat), 16 mg chol., 165 mg sodium, 24 g carb., 1 g fiber, 3 g pro.*

PREP 15 minutes
BAKE 12 minutes

16 servings	ingredients	32 servings
2 cups	all-purpose flour	4 cups
1 cup	yellow cornmeal	2 cups
2 Tbsp.	granulated sugar	¼ cup
1½ tsp.	baking powder	3 tsp.
½ tsp.	salt	1 tsp.
½ cup	cold butter, coarsely shredded* or cubed	1 cup
1 cup	buttermilk or sour milk**	2 cups
	Coarse sugar	

Farro and Kale Salad

Tuscan kale, also called lacinato kale (or dinosaur kale, for its nubby-texture leaves) is more tender than the more common curly leaf kale, making it a good choice for using raw in salads.

1. In a saucepan combine farro and 1½ cups water. Bring to boiling; reduce heat. Cover; simmer 30 minutes or until tender. Drain; rinse with cold water until cool.

2. Preheat oven to 350°F. In a shallow baking pan toss almonds with 1 tsp. oil, garlic salt, and pepper. Roast 10 to 12 minutes or until toasted, stirring once. Remove from oven; cool.

3. For dressing, in a screw-top jar combine 3 Tbsp. oil, lemon juice, and garlic. Add salt and pepper to taste. Cover; shake. In a large bowl toss kale with 1 Tbsp. dressing. Using clean hands, massage dressing into kale 15 seconds. Using vegetable peeler, cut ribbons from carrots. Add farro, carrots, nuts, berries, and cheese to kale. Add remaining dressing; toss to combine.

FOR 12 SERVINGS In Step 1, use a large saucepan and 3 cups water. In Step 2, use 2 tsp. oil. In Step 3, use 6 Tbsp. oil and toss kale with 2 Tbsp. dressing.

PER SERVING *216 cal., 13 g fat (2 g sat. fat), 5 mg chol., 123 mg sodium, 21 g carb., 5 g fiber, 6 g pro.*

COOK 30 minutes
PREP 30 minutes   **BAKE** 10 minutes

6 servings	ingredients	12 servings
½ cup	uncooked farro	1 cup
¼ cup	whole almonds	½ cup
1 tsp.	extra-virgin olive oil	2 tsp.
¼ tsp.	garlic salt	½ tsp.
¼ tsp.	freshly ground pepper	½ tsp.
3 Tbsp.	extra-virgin olive oil	¼ cup + 2 Tbsp.
3 Tbsp.	lemon juice	¼ cup + 2 Tbsp.
1	clove garlic, minced	2
½ lb.	Tuscan kale, stemmed and cut lengthwise into ¼-inch ribbons	1 lb.
3	small carrots, peeled	6
½ cup	blueberries	1 cup
¼ cup	shaved Kasseri or Havarti cheese	½ cup

Summer Corn and Tomato Salad with Bacon

Bacon makes everything, even peak-season tomatoes and sweet corn—better! This summery salad is delicious with burgers or grilled salmon.

1. Brush corn with 1 Tbsp. of the oil. Grill corn, covered, over medium-high heat 10 to 15 minutes or until browned, turning frequently. When cool enough to handle, cut kernels from cobs.

2. In a large bowl combine corn, tomatoes, onion, marjoram, and crumbled bacon. In a small bowl whisk together remaining oil, vinegar, salt, and pepper. Drizzle over salad; toss to combine.

FOR 12 SERVINGS In Step 1, use 2 Tbsp. oil.

PER SERVING *147 cal., 10 g fat (2 g sat. fat), 5 mg chol., 297 mg sodium, 14 g carb., 2 g fiber, 4 g pro.*

PREP 25 minutes
GRILL 10 minutes

6 servings	ingredients	12 servings
4	ears of corn, husks and silks removed	8
3 Tbsp.	olive oil	¼ cup + 2 Tbsp.
1 cup	cherry or grape tomatoes, halved	2 cups
¼ cup	finely chopped red onion	½ cup
¼ cup	chopped fresh marjoram, oregano, or parsley	½ cup
4 slices	bacon, crisp-cooked and crumbled	8 slices
2 Tbsp.	cider vinegar	¼ cup
½ tsp.	salt	1 tsp.
½ tsp.	freshly ground black pepper	1 tsp.

Chopped Green Bean Salad with Manchego

Golden raisins add a sweet element and Manchego—a Spanish sheep's milk cheese—a complementary tangy taste to this grain and green bean salad.

1. Prepare farro. Meanwhile, in a large pot cook green beans in lightly salted boiling water 4 minutes or until crisp-tender. Transfer beans with a slotted spoon to a bowl half-filled with ice water to stop cooking; drain and set aside. Meanwhile, finely shred 4 oz. of the cheese; cut remaining cheese into bite-size pieces.

2. For dressing, in a blender combine the vinegar, shallot, salt, and pepper. Add the shredded cheese and olive oil; cover and blend until well combined and creamy. In a large bowl combine the cooked beans, dressing, cheese pieces, almonds, raisins, and farro. Toss to combine.

*TIP For 2 cups cooked farro, in a medium saucepan combine ¾ cup uncooked farro and 1½ cups water. Bring to boiling; reduce heat. Cover; simmer 30 minutes or until tender. Drain, if necessary. For 3 cups cooked farro, use a large saucepan, 1⅛ cups uncooked farro, and 2¼ cups water.

FOR 12 SERVINGS In Step 1, finely shred 6 oz. of the cheese.

PER SERVING *392 cal., 25 g fat (7 g sat. fat), 21 mg chol., 335 mg sodium, 33 g carb., 6 g fiber, 12 g pro.*

START TO FINISH 30 minutes

8 servings	ingredients	12 servings
2 cups	cooked farro*	3 cups
1¼ lb.	green beans, trimmed and cut into 1-inch pieces	1¾ lb.
6 oz.	Manchego, Asiago, or Parmesan cheese	9 oz.
⅓ cup	red wine vinegar	½ cup
1	shallot, peeled and cut up	1
½ tsp.	salt	¾ tsp.
¼ tsp.	black pepper	½ tsp.
⅓ cup	extra-virgin olive oil	½ cup
¾ cup	toasted almonds, chopped	1 cup
¾ cup	golden raisins	1 cup

Double-Ginger Celery Salad

This super-refreshing salad has crunch coming from all sides—celery, apple, and pistachios. It goes particularly well with pork and chicken.

1. Trim and cut celery into 2- to 3-inch pieces, reserving leafy tops, if desired. Thinly slice pieces lengthwise.

2. In a large bowl whisk together apple cider vinegar, extra-virgin olive oil, ground ginger, and salt. Add celery, apple slices, pistachios, and chopped crystallized ginger. Toss to combine. If desired, top with some of the reserved leaves.

PER SERVING *133 cal., 11 g fat (1 g sat. fat), 0 mg chol., 151 mg sodium, 8 g carb., 2 g fiber, 2 g pro.*

START TO FINISH 25 minutes

8 servings	ingredients	16 servings
1 lb.	celery	2 lb.
¼ cup	apple cider vinegar	½ cup
¼ cup	extra-virgin olive oil	½ cup
½ tsp.	ground ginger	1 tsp.
½ tsp.	kosher salt	1 tsp.
1	Honeycrisp or Jazz apple, cored and thinly sliced	2
½ cup	chopped roasted, salted shelled pistachios	1 cup
3 Tbsp.	chopped crystallized ginger	¼ cup + 2 Tbsp.

Vinaigrette Coleslaw

Classic creamy coleslaw may be the standard side to traditional barbecue, but sometimes you want something a little lighter. When you do, try this refreshing rainbow-color slaw.

1. For vinaigrette, in a screw-top jar combine first seven ingredients (through pepper). Cover and shake well.

2. In a large bowl combine remaining ingredients. Pour vinaigrette over cabbage mixture; toss gently to coat. Cover and chill 2 to 24 hours.

PER SERVING *79 cal., 5 g fat (0 g sat. fat), 0 mg chol., 120 mg sodium, 10 g carb., 2 g fiber, 1 g pro.*

PREP 20 minutes
CHILL 2 hours

6 servings	ingredients	12 servings
3 Tbsp.	cider vinegar	¼ cup + 2 Tbsp.
2 Tbsp.	sugar	¼ cup
2 Tbsp.	vegetable oil	¼ cup
½ tsp.	celery seeds or caraway seeds (optional)	1 tsp.
¼ tsp.	salt	½ tsp.
¼ tsp.	dry mustard	½ tsp.
⅛ to ¼ tsp.	black pepper	¼ to ½ tsp.
5 cups	coleslaw mix	10 cups
¼ cup	thinly sliced green onions	½ cup

Cucumber-Honeydew Salad with Feta

When ripe, honeydew is very sweet (hence its name) with a hint of floral flavor. Together with the clean freshness of cucumber and the tanginess of feta cheese, they create a perfect balance.

START TO FINISH 20 minutes

10 servings	ingredients	20 servings
2 Tbsp.	lemon juice	¼ cup
¼ cup	olive oil	½ cup
1 tsp.	honey	2 tsp.
¼ tsp.	salt	½ tsp.
¼ tsp.	poppy seeds (optional)	½ tsp.
⅛ tsp.	black pepper	¼ tsp.
5 cups	seeded and cubed honeydew melon	10 cups
2 cups	chopped, unpeeled cucumber	4 cups
⅓ cup	finely chopped red onion	⅔ cup
3 Tbsp.	snipped fresh dill	¼ cup + 2 Tbsp.
1 cup	crumbled feta cheese	2 cups

1. For dressing, pour lemon juice into a large bowl. Gradually add oil in a steady stream, whisking until incorporated. Whisk in honey, salt, poppy seeds (if using), and pepper until combined.

2. Add honeydew melon, cucumber, and red onion, to bowl; toss gently to coat. Top with cheese and dill just before serving.

*TO MAKE AHEAD Prepare dressing through Step 1. Cover and chill up to 8 hours. Let stand at room temperature 20 minutes. Mix with fruit and vegetables just before serving. Top with cheese and dill.

PER SERVING *118 cal., 8 g fat (2 g sat. fat), 10 mg chol., 202 mg sodium, 11 g carb., 1 g fiber, 2 g pro.*

Spicy Fruit Salad

In Mexico, fruits such as mango and coconut and vegetables such as cucumber and jicama are eaten as a snack sprinkled with lime, chili powder, and salt. This colorful salad extrapolates that idea to a full-blown side dish.

START TO FINISH 35 minutes

10 servings	ingredients	20 servings
6 cups	shredded romaine lettuce	12 cups
3 cups	arugula	6 cups
3 (3 cups)	mangoes, seeded, peeled, and sliced	6 (6 cups)
3 cups	fresh strawberries, halved	6 cups
1 cup	jicama matchsticks	2 cups
¼ cup	vegetable oil	½ cup
3 Tbsp.	lime juice	¼ cup + 2 Tbsp.
1 Tbsp.	honey	2 Tbsp.
1 tsp.	chili powder	2 tsp.
1 tsp.	adobo sauce (from a can of chipotles in adobo sauce)	2 tsp.
¼ tsp.	kosher salt	½ tsp.
	Sliced jalapeño peppers (tip, page 15)	

1. In a 4-qt. clear salad or trifle bowl layer romaine, arugula, mangoes, strawberries, and jicama. (May be covered tightly and chilled up to 4 hours.)

2. For the dressing, whisk together oil, lime juice, honey, chili powder, adobo sauce, and salt. Drizzle dressing over salad; top with jalapeño slices.

FOR 20 SERVINGS In Step 1, use two 4-qt. clear salad or trifle bowls.

PER SERVING *119 cal., 6 g fat (1 g sat. fat), 0 mg chol., 114 mg sodium, 18 g carb., 3 g fiber, 2 g pro.*

Peach and Tomato Salad

Although it's tempting to buy those pretty peaches that appear in the supermarket in midsummer (or even earlier!), you risk being disappointed in their flavor and texture. For the sweetest, juiciest peaches, it's best to wait until mid-August and enjoy them through the end of the season, usually in late September.

1. In an extra-large bowl whisk together vinegar, oil, honey, salt, and black pepper. Add peaches, tomatoes, red onion, cheese, and pecans; toss to coat. Top with basil. Serve immediately.

PER SERVING *192 cal., 13 g fat (3 g sat. fat), 11 mg chol., 219 mg sodium, 16 g carb., 3 g fiber, 4 g pro.*

START TO FINISH 30 minutes

6 servings	ingredients	12 servings
¼ cup	balsamic vinegar	½ cup
2 Tbsp.	olive oil	¼ cup
1½ tsp.	honey	1 Tbsp.
¼ tsp.	salt	½ tsp.
¼ tsp.	black pepper	½ tsp.
3	medium ripe peaches, pitted and cut into wedges	6
1 lb.	tomatoes, cut into wedges and/or cherry tomatoes, halved	2 lb.
½ cup	thinly sliced red onion	1 cup
½ cup	crumbled feta cheese	1 cup
½ cup	pecan halves, toasted (tip, page 89)	1 cup
¼ cup	torn fresh basil	½ cup

CHAPTER 6

Desserts

When you're looking to make a sweet to share, these cakes, cookies, bars, or fruit desserts will bring smiles to the faces of your friends and family.

166

168

180

Peanut Butter Chip Oatmeal Cake

This cinnamon-spiced snack cake goes together super fast—perfect for when you need something sweet in a hurry.

1. Preheat oven to 350°F. In a large bowl combine boiling water and oats; let stand 10 minutes. Meanwhile, grease an 8-inch baking pan.

2. Add both sugars and butter to oats mixture, stirring until butter is melted. Stir in egg until combined. Stir in flour, baking soda, cinnamon, and salt. Stir in 1 cup of the peanut butter pieces.

3. Spread batter in prepared pan. Sprinkle with pecans and remaining peanut butter pieces. Bake 35 minutes or until a toothpick inserted near center comes out clean. Cool in pan on a wire rack. If desired, drizzle with warmed peanut butter and/or grape jelly.

FOR 20 SERVINGS In Step 1, use a 13×9-inch baking pan. In Step 2, stir in 2 cups of the peanut butter pieces.

PER SERVING *274 cal., 13 g fat (7 g sat. fat), 31 mg chol., 196 mg sodium, 36 g carb., 2 g fiber, 6 g pro.*

PREP 25 minutes
BAKE 35 minutes

10 servings	ingredients	20 servings
7 oz.	boiling water	14 oz.
½ cup	quick-cooking rolled oats	1 cup
½ cup	granulated sugar	1 cup
½ cup	packed brown sugar	1 cup
¼ cup	butter, cut up and softened	½ cup
1	egg	2
¾ cup + 2 Tbsp.	all-purpose flour	1¾ cups
½ tsp.	baking soda	1 tsp.
½ tsp.	ground cinnamon	1 tsp.
¼ tsp.	salt	½ tsp.
half 10-oz. pkg.	peanut butter-flavor pieces	one 10-oz. pkg.
⅓ cup	chopped pecans	⅔ cup
	Peanut butter and/or grape jelly, warmed (optional)	

Maple Butter Cake

PREP 25 minutes
BAKE 40 minutes

12 servings	ingredients	24 servings
2 cups	all-purpose flour	4 cups
3 Tbsp.	granulated sugar	6 Tbsp.
½ tsp.	ground cinnamon	1 tsp.
⅓ cup	cold butter	⅔ cup
¾ cup	butter, softened	1½ cups
¾ cup	granulated sugar	1½ cups
1	egg	2
⅔ cup	pure maple syrup	1⅓ cups
½ cup	half-and-half	1 cup
	Powdered sugar and/or maple syrup (optional)	

Pure maple syrup is a pricey but necessary ingredient in this cake for the best results. Don't be tempted to use maple-flavor syrup, which is mostly corn syrup.

1. Preheat oven to 350°F. In a medium bowl combine 1 cup flour, 3 Tbsp. granulated sugar, and the cinnamon. Use a pastry blender to cut in the cold butter until mixture resembles fine crumbs and starts to cling together. Pat into the bottom of a 9-inch baking pan. Bake 5 minutes or just until set.

2. In a large bowl beat the softened butter with a mixer on medium 30 seconds. Add ¾ cup granulated sugar and beat until combined. Beat in egg and maple syrup. Alternately, add remaining 1 cup flour and half-and-half, beating on low after each addition just until combined (batter may appear slightly curdled). Pour into crust-lined baking pan.

3. Bake 35 minutes or until the cake is nearly firm when gently shaken. Cool in pan on a wire rack. If desired, sift powdered sugar over top and serve with additional maple syrup.

FOR 24 SERVINGS In Step 1, use 2 cups flour and 6 Tbsp. sugar. Use a 9×13-inch baking pan. In Step 2, use 1½ cups sugar and 2 cups flour.

PER SERVING *348 cal., 18 g fat (11 g sat. fat), 3 mg chol., 147 mg sodium, 44 g carb., 1 g fiber, 3 g pro.*

Candy Bar Cupcakes

20 servings	ingredients	40 servings
1½ cups	all-purpose flour	3 cups
2 tsp.	baking powder	4 tsp.
½ tsp.	baking soda	1 tsp.
½ tsp.	salt	1 tsp.
⅓ cup	butter, softened	⅔ cup
⅓ cup	peanut butter	⅔ cup
1 cup	packed brown sugar	2 cups
2	eggs	4
1 tsp.	vanilla	2 tsp.
1 cup	buttermilk	2 cups
1 cup	chopped chocolate-coated caramel-topped nougat bars with peanuts	2 cups
¾ cup	butter, softened	1½ cups
8 cups	powdered sugar	16 cups
½ cup	caramel sauce	1 cup
¼ tsp.	salt	½ tsp.
¼ cup	milk	½ cup
1 cup	semisweet chocolate chips, melted (optional)	2 cups

Can't decide if you want a dessert with chocolate, caramel, or nuts? These cupcakes have all three—in the form of chopped candy bars in the batter and as a topping on the frosting.

1. Preheat oven to 350°F. Line twenty to twenty-two 2½-inch muffin cups with paper bake cups. In a bowl stir together flour, baking powder, baking soda, and salt.

2. In a large bowl beat the ⅓ cup butter and peanut butter with a mixer on medium 30 seconds. Add brown sugar, ¼ cup at a time, beating until combined. Scrape bowl; beat 2 minutes more. Add eggs, one at a time, beating after each addition. Beat in vanilla. Alternately, add flour mixture and buttermilk, beating on low after each addition until combined. Stir in chopped candy bars. Spoon batter into prepared muffin cups, filling each two-thirds full.

3. Bake 18 to 20 minutes or until a toothpick inserted near center comes out clean. Cool in muffin cups on a wire rack 5 minutes. Remove from muffin cups; cool on wire rack.

4. Meanwhile, for caramel frosting, in a large bowl beat ¾ cup butter with a mixer until smooth. Gradually add 2 cups of the powdered sugar, beating well. Slowly beat in caramel sauce and salt. Gradually beat in remaining powdered sugar. Beat in enough milk to make piping consistency.

5. Spoon caramel frosting into a decorating bag fitted with a large star tip. Pipe frosting onto cupcakes. If desired, drizzle with melted chocolate and top with additional chopped candy bars.

FOR 40 SERVINGS In Step 1, use forty to forty-four 2½-inch muffin cups with paper bake cups. In Step 2, use ⅔ cup butter. In Step 4, use 1½ cups butter; add 4 cups powdered sugar.

PER SERVING *465 cal., 15 g fat (8 g sat. fat), 47 mg chol., 336 mg sodium, 80 g carb., 1 g fiber, 4 g pro.*

Mocha Tres Leches

Tres leches ("three milks") cake is a popular dessert throughout Latin America. The name refers to a sauce made with evaporated milk, sweetened condensed milk, and fresh milk or cream. When the cake has been baked and cooled, the top is poked with a fork and the sauce is poured on top to saturate the cake. This version adds mocha to the mix.

PREP 40 minutes　**BAKE** 30 minutes
COOL 1 hour　**CHILL** 3 hours

8 servings	ingredients	16 servings
3	eggs	6
6 Tbsp.	milk	¾ cup
6 Tbsp.	unsweetened cocoa powder	¾ cup
¾ cup + 2 Tbsp.	all-purpose flour	1¾ cups
2 tsp.	baking powder	4 tsp.
½ tsp.	salt	1 tsp.
¾ cup	granulated sugar	1½ cups
1 tsp.	vanilla	2 tsp.
half 12-oz. can	evaporated milk	one 12-oz. can
1½ Tbsp.	instant espresso coffee powder	3 Tbsp.
1 cup + 2 Tbsp.	heavy cream	2¼ cups
half 14-oz. can	sweetened condensed milk	one 14-oz. can
2 oz.	cream cheese, softened	4 oz.
½ cup	powdered sugar	1 cup
	Chocolate jimmies (optional)	

1. Preheat oven to 325°F. Separate eggs, placing egg whites in a large bowl and yolks in a small bowl; set aside. In a saucepan heat milk over medium heat until simmering; remove from heat. Whisk in the cocoa powder. Cool.

2. In a bowl combine flour and baking powder. Beat egg whites and salt with a mixer on medium until frothy. Increase to medium-high and beat until soft peaks form (tips curl). Slowly add granulated sugar, beating until stiff peaks form (tips stand straight).

3. Add egg yolks to beaten whites just until combined. Alternately, add flour mixture and cooled chocolate mixture to egg mixture, beating well after each addition. Add vanilla; beat just until combined.

4. Pour batter into an ungreased 8-inch baking pan. Bake 30 minutes or until a wooden toothpick inserted near the center comes out clean. Cool in pan on a wire rack 1 hour.

5. In a saucepan combine the evaporated milk and espresso powder. Heat and stir over medium heat until espresso is dissolved. Remove from heat. Stir in ⅓ cup heavy cream and sweetened condensed milk. Using fork tines, poke holes in cake. Pour espresso mixture over cake.

6. Meanwhile, in a bowl beat cream cheese with a mixer on medium until smooth; beat in the powdered sugar. Add 2 Tbsp. heavy cream; beat until combined. Add the remaining heavy cream; beat until soft peaks form (tips curl).

7. Spread whipped cream over cake. Chill 3 hours or up to 24 hours. If desired, sprinkle with chocolate jimmies.

FOR 16 SERVINGS Use an ungreased 9×13-inch baking pan. In Step 5, stir in ⅔ cup heavy cream. In Step 6, add ¼ cup heavy cream, then the remaining cream.

PER SERVING *447 cal., 21 g fat (12 g sat. fat), 139 mg chol., 360 mg sodium, 57 g carb., 2 g fiber, 10 g pro.*

Caramel-S'mores Cake

Grilled pound cake stands in for the graham crackers in this "fancified" take on s'mores. Kids can still help make it, though—have the littlest ones unwrap the caramels and the older ones toast the marshmallows.

1. If using wooden skewers, soak in water 30 minutes. For chocolate sauce, in a small bowl microwave chocolate, cream, and, if desired, liqueur 1 to 1½ minutes or until chocolate is softened. Stir until smooth. Thread marshmallows onto four 12-inch skewers. Brush cake slices with melted butter.

2. Grease grill rack. Grill cake, uncovered, over medium heat 1 to 2 minutes or until toasted, turning once. Remove from grill.

3. For the caramel sauce, in a saucepan stir caramels and heavy cream over low heat until smooth.

4. Holding marshmallow kabobs just above grill rack, grill 3 to 4 minutes, turning as needed to soften marshmallows and brown all sides.

5. Spoon chocolate sauce onto cake slices. Top with marshmallows, caramel sauce and, if desired, crumbled graham crackers.

FOR 8 SERVINGS In Step 1, use eight skewers.

PER SERVING *581 cal., 30 g fat (19 g sat. fat), 85 mg chol., 250 mg sodium, 77 g carb., 2 g fiber, 6 g pro.*

START TO FINISH 25 minutes

4 servings	ingredients	8 servings
½ cup	semisweet chocolate pieces	1 cup
3 Tbsp.	heavy cream	¼ cup + 2 Tbsp.
1 Tbsp.	coffee liqueur (optional)	2 Tbsp.
12	marshmallows	24
four ¾-inch slices	prepared or frozen pound cake, thawed	eight ¾-inch slices
1 Tbsp.	butter, melted	2 Tbsp.
18	unwrapped vanilla caramels	36
3 Tbsp.	heavy cream	¼ cup + 2 Tbsp.
4 squares	graham crackers, coarsely crumbled (optional)	8 squares

Cinnamon Roll-Apple Pie Bake

You can pick the kind of apple you like from the ingredients list depending on the flavor of apple you like. Golden Delicious is the sweetest and Granny Smith the most tart—and everything else somewhere in between!

1. Preheat oven to 350° F. In an extra-large bowl stir together sugar, flour, and ginger. Add apples, raisins, and water; toss to combine. Spoon apple mixture into a 2-qt. round casserole dish; cover. Place a foil-lined baking sheet on oven rack below casserole dish. Bake, covered, 50 minutes or until apples begin to soften.

2. Arrange cinnamon roll pieces on apple filling. Bake, uncovered, 25 to 30 minutes or until rolls are golden. Cool at least 30 minutes. Drizzle icing from cinnamon roll package over top.

TIP If you don't have a 2-qt. casserole, use a 2-qt. square baking dish. Prepare as directed, covering dish with foil and reducing baking time to 40 minutes in Step 1. Continue as directed in Step 2.

FOR 16 SERVINGS In Step 1, use a 3.2- to 4-qt. casserole.

PER SERVING *316 cal., 6 g fat (1 g sat. fat), 0 mg chol., 409 mg sodium, 65 g carb., 3 g fiber, 3 g pro.*

PREP 30 minutes
BAKE 1 hour 15 minutes **COOL** 30 minutes

8 servings	ingredients	16 servings
½ cup	sugar	1 cup
2 Tbsp.	all-purpose flour	¼ cup
1 tsp.	ground ginger	2 tsp.
7 cups	peeled, cored, and sliced apples (Braeburn, Piñata, Granny Smith, Idared, and/or Golden Delicious)	14 cups
¼ cup	golden raisins	½ cup
¼ cup	water	½ cup
one 17.5-oz. pkg. (5)	refrigerated large cinnamon rolls with icing, quartered	two 17.5-oz. pkg. (10)

Blueberry Cobbler with Lemon-Poppyseed Scones

Blueberry and lemon are often paired together— lemon enhances the flavor of blueberries. This warm dessert features buttery lemon scones on top of a bubbling blueberry filling.

PREP 30 minutes
BAKE 40 minutes

8 servings	ingredients	16 servings
1¼ cups	all-purpose flour	2½ cups
¼ cup	sugar	½ cup
1½ tsp.	baking powder	3 tsp.
1½ tsp.	lemon zest	3 tsp.
1½ Tbsp.	poppy seeds	3 Tbsp.
¼ tsp.	salt	½ tsp.
½ cup	butter, cut into cubes	1 cup
½ cup	heavy cream	1 cup
1	egg, lightly beaten	2
3 Tbsp.	sugar	¼ cup + 2 Tbsp.
1 tsp.	cornstarch	2 tsp.
3 cups	fresh blueberries	6 cups
¼ cup	orange-flavor liqueur (such as Cointreau) or orange juice	½ cup

1. Preheat oven to 375°F. In a bowl combine the first six ingredients (through salt). Add butter to flour mixture. Beat with mixer on low until pea-size crumbs form. Add cream all at once to flour mixture. Stir just until dry ingredients are moistened.

2. Turn dough out onto a lightly floured surface; knead dough by folding and gently pressing three to four strokes, just until dough comes together. Pat dough into an eight-inch square. Cut square in half diagonally each way. Cut each quarter in half to make a total of 8 triangles. Brush with beaten egg. If desired, sprinkle with additional sugar.

3. Grease a 2-qt. square baking dish. In a large bowl combine 3 Tbsp. sugar and the cornstarch. Add blueberries and liqueur and toss gently. Transfer to prepared baking dish. Arrange scones on blueberries. Bake 40 to 45 minutes or until berries are bubbly and scones are golden brown. Cool slightly; serve warm.

FOR 16 SERVINGS In Step 2, divide dough in half. Pat each half in an 8-inch square. Cut square in half diagonally each way. Cut each quarter in half to make a total of 16 triangles. In Step 3, use a 3-qt. baking dish and 6 Tbsp. sugar.

PER SERVING *337 cal., 19 g fat (11 g sat. fat), 71 mg chol., 270 mg sodium, 38 g carb., 2 g fiber, 4 g pro.*

Honey-Pistachio Roasted Pears

When you are looking for a dessert on the light side, this is a lovely choice. It's best in the fall, when pears are at peak season.

1. Preheat oven to 400°F. Arrange pears, cut sides down, in a 2-qt. rectangular baking dish. Add the next four ingredients (through orange zest). Roast, uncovered, 20 to 25 minutes or until tender, spooning liquid over pears occasionally.

2. Transfer pears to serving dishes with some of the liquid. Stir together mascarpone cheese and powdered sugar. Spoon over pears; sprinkle with pistachios. If desired, drizzle with additional honey.

*TIP Choose firm, but ripe pears.

FOR 12 SERVINGS In Step 1, use a 3-qt. rectangular baking dish.

PER SERVING *250 cal., 15 g fat (8 g sat. fat), 37 mg chol., 69 mg sodium, 27 g carb., 3 g fiber, 3 g pro.*

PREP 20 minutes
ROAST 20 minutes

6 servings	ingredients	12 servings
3	ripe medium Bosc or Bartlett pears,* peeled, halved, and cored	6
¼ cup	pear nectar	½ cup
3 Tbsp.	honey	¼ cup + 2 Tbsp.
2 Tbsp.	butter	4 Tbsp.
1 tsp.	orange zest	2 tsp.
½ cup	mascarpone cheese	1 cup
2 Tbsp.	powdered sugar	¼ cup
⅓ cup	chopped roasted, salted pistachios	⅔ cup

Sweet Ricotta and Strawberry Parfaits

When strawberries are at their ripest, sweetest, and red all of the way through, layer them with sweetened ricotta for a perfect summer dessert.

PREP 20 minutes
STAND 15 minutes

6 servings	ingredients	12 servings
1 lb.	fresh strawberries, hulled and halved or quartered	2 lb.
1 Tbsp.	snipped fresh mint	2 Tbsp.
1 tsp.	sugar	2 tsp.
one 15-oz. carton	part-skim ricotta cheese	two 15-oz. cartons
3 Tbsp.	honey	¼ cup + 2 Tbsp.
½ tsp.	vanilla	1 tsp.
¼ tsp.	lemon zest	½ tsp.

1. In a medium bowl gently stir together strawberries, mint, and sugar. Let stand 15 minutes or until berries are softened and starting to release their juices.

2. In a medium bowl beat the remaining ingredients with a mixer on medium 2 minutes.

3. To assemble parfaits, scoop 2 Tbsp. of the ricotta mixture into each of six parfait glasses. Top each with a large spoonful of strawberry mixture. Repeat layers. If desired, top with additional fresh mint and whole strawberries. Serve immediately or cover and chill up to 4 hours.

FOR 12 SERVINGS Use 12 parfait glasses.

PER SERVING *159 cal., 6 g fat (4 g sat. fat), 22 mg chol., 90 mg sodium, 18 g carb., 2 g fiber, 9 g pro.*

Cherry Pie Bites

These two-bite cherry pies are small enough you don't have to feel guilty about having more than one. And with a buttery cream-cheese crust, sweet-tart filling and streusel topping, you will want to.

PREP 30 minutes
BAKE 25 minutes **COOL** 5 minutes

24 servings	ingredients	48 servings
½ cup	butter, softened	1 cup
one 3-oz. pkg.	cream cheese, softened	one 6-oz. pkg.
1 cup + 2 Tbsp.	all-purpose flour	2 cups + ¼ cup
2 Tbsp.	chopped toasted walnuts or pecans (tip, page. 8)	¼ cup
2 Tbsp.	packed brown sugar	¼ cup
⅛ tsp.	ground nutmeg	¼ tsp.
1½ Tbsp.	butter	3 Tbsp.
2 cups	fresh or frozen unsweetened pitted tart red cherries, thawed	4 cups
⅓ cup	granulated sugar	⅔ cup
2 tsp.	cornstarch	4 tsp.

1. Preheat oven to 325°F. In a medium bowl beat the ½ cup butter and cream cheese with a mixer on medium to high until combined. Stir in 1 cup of the flour. Shape dough into 24 balls. Press the balls into the bottoms and up the sides of 24 ungreased 1¾-inch muffin cups.

2. For streusel, in a small bowl stir together the remaining flour, nuts, brown sugar, and nutmeg. Using a pastry blender, cut in the 1½ Tbsp. butter until mixture is crumbly.

3. For filling, in a small saucepan combine the cherries, granulated sugar, and cornstarch. Cook over medium heat until cherries release juices, stirring occasionally. Continue to cook, stirring constantly, over medium heat until thick and bubbly. Spoon about 1 heaping tsp. of the filling into each pastry-lined cup. Evenly sprinkle filled cups with streusel.

4. Bake 25 to 30 minutes or until edges are light brown. Cool in pan on a wire rack 5 minutes. Carefully remove bites from pan; cool on wire rack.

FOR 48 SERVINGS In Step 1, use 1 cup butter and 2 cups flour. Shape dough in 48 balls and use 48 ungreased 1¾-inch muffin cups. In Step 2, cut in 3 Tbsp. butter.

PER SERVING *100 cal., 6 g fat (4 g sat. fat), 16 mg chol., 52 mg sodium, 10 g carb., 0 g fiber, 1 g pro.*

Minty Cookies and Cream Tassies

For an investment of just 20 minutes, you can make these sweet (and pretty!) little bites. They call for chopped chocolate sandwich cookies and mini phyllo dough shells to keep things easy-peasy.

1. In a medium bowl beat heavy cream and vanilla with a mixer on medium to high until soft peaks form (tips curl). Add cream cheese and sugar, beating until combined. Beat in crème de menthe.

2. Divide the chopped cookies among phyllo shells. Top with cream cheese mixture. If desired, top each tassie with a halved cookie.

*TIP For 30 tassies, you can substitute 1 Tbsp. milk and ½ tsp. mint extract. For 60 tassies, use 2 Tbsp. milk and 1 tsp. mint extract.

PER SERVING *57 cal., 3 g fat (1 g sat. fat), 7 mg chol., 31 mg sodium, 5 g carb., 0 g fiber, 1 g pro.*

START TO FINISH 20 minutes

30 servings	ingredients	60 servings
¼ cup	heavy cream	½ cup
½ tsp.	vanilla	1 tsp.
4 oz.	cream cheese, softened	8 oz.
3 Tbsp.	sugar	¼ cup + 2 Tbsp.
1 Tbsp.	green or white crème de menthe liqueur*	2 Tbsp.
¾ cup	chopped chocolate sandwich cookies with white filling	1½ cups
30	baked miniature phyllo dough shells	60
15	chocolate sandwich cookies with white filling, halved (optional)	30

Lemon-Cream Icebox Cookie Sandwiches

Attention, lemon lovers! There's a double dose of this favorite flavor in these yummy sandwich cookies. It's in the buttery cookies as well as the cream cheese-and-butter filling. They're perfect for enjoying with a cup of tea.

1. For the cookies, in a large bowl beat shortening and butter with a mixer on medium to high 30 seconds. Add granulated sugar, baking powder, and salt. Beat until combined, scraping bowl as needed. Beat in egg and vanilla. Beat in flour. Stir in the 2 tsp. lemon zest.

2. Divide dough in half. Shape each half into a 10-inch roll. If desired, coat rolls in decorating sugar. Wrap each in plastic wrap or waxed paper; chill until firm enough to slice (1 to 2 hours).

3. Preheat oven to 375°F. Use a serrated knife to cut rolls into ⅛-inch slices; place 2 inches apart on an ungreased cookie sheet. Bake 8 to 10 minutes or until set. Cool on cookie sheet 1 minute. Remove; cool on a wire rack.

4. For lemon-cream frosting, in a large bowl beat cream cheese and butter with a mixer on medium until smooth. Gradually beat in powdered sugar until combined. Stir in 1 Tbsp. lemon zest.

5. Spread about 1 Tbsp. lemon-cream frosting onto bottoms of half the cookies. Top with remaining cookies, bottom sides down. If desired, roll edges of sandwich cookies in additional decorating sugar. Chill 1 hour or until frosting is set.

FOR 100 SERVINGS In Step 1, use 4 tsp. lemon zest. In Step 2, divide dough in fourths. In Step 4, use 2 Tbsp. lemon zest.

PER SERVING *140 cal., 8 g fat (4 g sat. fat), 20 mg chol., 76 mg sodium, 17 g carb., 0 g fiber, 1 g pro.*

PREP 30 minutes
CHILL 2 hours   **BAKE** 8 minutes per batch

50 servings	ingredients	100 servings
½ cup	shortening	1 cup
½ cup	butter, softened	1 cup
1 cup	granulated sugar	2 cups
1 tsp.	baking powder	2 tsp.
¼ tsp.	salt	½ tsp.
1	egg	2
1 tsp.	vanilla	2 tsp.
2¼ cups	all-purpose flour	4½ cups
2 tsp.	lemon zest	4 tsp.
	Yellow decorating sugar (optional)	
one 8-oz. pkg.	cream cheese, softened	two 8-oz. pkg.
⅔ cup	butter, softened	1⅓ cups
3⅓ cups	powdered sugar	6⅔ cups
1 Tbsp.	lemon zest	2 Tbsp.

Cinnamon Roll Cookies

The trick to keeping these cookies perfectly round and tightly spiraled is to freeze the filled dough roll at least 30 minutes or until it is firm enough to slice without getting smashed.

PREP 30 minutes **CHILL** 30 minutes
FREEZE 30 minutes **BAKE** 8 minutes per batch

40 servings	ingredients	80 servings
1 cup	butter, softened	2 cups
⅔ cup	sugar	1⅓ cups
½ tsp.	salt	1 tsp.
1	egg	2
1 Tbsp.	vanilla	2 Tbsp.
2 cups	all-purpose flour	4 cups
1	egg, lightly beaten	2
½ cup	packed brown sugar	1 cup
2 tsp.	ground cinnamon, pumpkin pie spice, or apple pie spice	4 tsp.
2 oz.	cream cheese, softened	4 oz.
1 Tbsp.	butter, softened	2 Tbsp.
¾ cup	powdered sugar	1½ cups
2 to 3 Tbsp.	milk	4 to 6 Tbsp.

1. In a large bowl beat butter with a mixer on medium to high 30 seconds. Add the sugar and salt. Beat on medium 2 minutes, scraping bowl as needed. Beat in egg and vanilla. Beat in flour.

2. Wrap dough in plastic wrap; chill until easy to handle (30 to 60 minutes). On a floured surface, roll dough to a 15×10-inch rectangle. Brush with the lightly beaten egg. Stir together brown sugar and cinnamon; sprinkle over dough. Roll up from a long side. Place rolls on a baking sheet or tray, cover, and freeze 30 minutes or until firm enough to slice.

3. Preheat oven to 375°F. Line a baking sheet with parchment paper. Use a serrated knife to cut roll into ¼-inch slices; place 2 inches apart on prepared sheet.

4. Bake 8 to 10 minutes or until edges are light brown. Cool on sheet 1 minute. Remove; cool on wire rack.

5. Meanwhile, for cream cheese icing, in a bowl beat cream cheese and butter with a mixer on medium until smooth. Beat in powdered sugar and enough milk to be spreadable. Spread cooled cookies with cream cheese icing.

FOR 80 SERVINGS In Step 2, roll half the dough at a time into a 15×10-inch rectangle, making two rolls.

PER SERVING *108 cal., 6 g fat (3 g sat. fat), 24 mg chol., 77 mg sodium, 13 g carb., 0 g fiber, 1 g pro.*

PB & J Sandwich Cookies

Choose your favorite jelly, jam, or preserves to fill these cookies. You can use either creamy or crunchy peanut butter, depending on whether you want the cookies studded with nuts.

PREP 30 minutes
BAKE 7 minutes per batch

40 servings	ingredients	80 servings
½ cup	shortening	1 cup
½ cup	peanut butter	1 cup
½ cup	granulated sugar	1 cup
½ cup	packed brown sugar	1 cup
1 tsp.	baking powder	2 tsp.
¼ tsp.	salt	½ tsp.
⅛ tsp.	baking soda	¼ tsp.
1	egg	2
2 Tbsp.	milk	¼ cup
1 tsp.	vanilla	2 tsp.
2 cups	all-purpose flour	4 cups
2 Tbsp.	granulated sugar	¼ cup
½ cup	jelly, jam, or preserves (any flavor)	1 cup

1. Preheat oven to 350°F. In a large bowl beat shortening and peanut butter with a mixer on medium to high 30 seconds. Add the ½ cup granulated sugar, the brown sugar, baking powder, salt, and baking soda. Beat until combined, scraping bowl as needed. Beat in egg, milk, and vanilla until combined. Beat in flour.

2. Shape dough into 1-inch balls. Roll balls in the 2 Tbsp. granulated sugar. Place 2 inches apart on an ungreased cookie sheet. Flatten slightly making crisscross marks with fork tines. Bake 7 to 9 minutes or until edges are firm and bottoms are light brown. Remove; cool cookies on wire rack.

3. For each sandwich cookie, spread bottom of one cookie with ½ tsp. jelly and, if desired, the bottom of another cookie with ½ tsp. peanut butter. Place one cookie on top of another, pressing together lightly.

FOR 80 SERVINGS In Step 1, use 1 cup sugar. In Step 2, use ¼ cup sugar.

PER SERVING *99 cal., 4 g fat (1 g sat. fat), 5 mg chol., 49 mg sodium, 14 g carb., 0 g fiber, 2 g pro.*

Chocolate, Coconut, and Almond Bars

These crunchy no-bake treats are made in the microwave, so there's no heating up the kitchen with the oven and no pan to wash by hand.

1. Line a 9-inch square pan with foil, extending foil over edges of pan. Butter foil.

2. In a large microwave-safe bowl microwave marshmallows and butter 1 to 2 minutes or until melted. Stir in coconut flavoring. Stir in the next three ingredients (through almonds). Cool slightly. Gently fold in chocolate pieces. Press mixture lightly onto bottom of prepared pan. Let stand about 1 hour or until set.

3. Using edges of foil, lift uncut bars out of pan. Cut into bars.

FOR 64 SERVINGS Use a 9×13-inch baking pan.

PER SERVING *147 cal., 8 g fat (4 g sat. fat), 3 mg chol., 55 mg sodium, 18 g carb., 1 g fiber, 2 g pro.*

PREP 20 minutes
STAND 1 hour

32 servings	ingredients	64 servings
one 10-oz. pkg.	large marshmallows	two 10-oz. pkg.
3 Tbsp.	butter, softened	6 Tbsp.
½ tsp.	coconut flavoring	1 tsp.
2 cups	sweetened flaked coconut	4 cups
2 cups	crispy flake and crunchy oat cluster cereal with honey and almonds	4 cups
1⅓ cups	honey-roasted flavor sliced almonds	2⅔ cups
1 cup	miniature semisweet chocolate pieces	2 cups

Gianduja-Cheesecake Brownies

The Swiss put a name to the magical combination of chocolate and hazelnut—gianduja [zhan-DOO-yah]. It's in spread form in these gooey brownies, but also comes in milk chocolate and bittersweet chocolate for eating out of hand.

1. Preheat oven to 325°F. Grease and lightly flour an 8-inch baking pan.

2. In a medium bowl stir together flour and cocoa powder. In a large bowl beat two of the eggs, 1 cup of the sugar, ¼ cup of the chocolate-hazelnut spread, and the melted butter with a mixer on low to medium until combined. Add flour mixture; stir until smooth. Spread batter in the prepared baking pan.

3. Wash beaters. In a large bowl beat the remaining eggs, remaining sugar, remaining chocolate-hazelnut spread, and cream cheese on medium until combined. Carefully spread over batter in pan.

4. Bake 50 to 55 minutes or until cream cheese layer is firm and set. Cool in pan on a wire rack. Cover and chill at least 1 hour before cutting. If desired, sprinkle brownies with additional cocoa powder.

FOR 32 SERVINGS In Step 1, use a 9×13-inch baking pan. In Step 2, beat 4 eggs, 2 cups sugar, and ½ cup chocolate-hazelnut spread.

PER SERVING *268 cal., 15 g fat, 76 mg chol., 134 mg sodium, 29 g carb., 1 g fiber, 5 g pro.*

PREP 25 minutes
BAKE 50 minutes   **CHILL** 1 hour

16 servings	ingredients	32 servings
2 cups	all-purpose flour	4 cups
¼ cup	unsweetened Dutch-process cocoa powder	½ cup
4	eggs	8
1 cup + 2 Tbsp.	sugar	2¼ cups
half 13-oz. jar	chocolate-hazelnut spread	one 13-oz. jar
½ cup + 2 Tbsp.	butter, melted and cooled	1¼ cups
one 8-oz. pkg.	reduced-fat cream cheese (neufchâtel), softened	two 8-oz. pkg.

Dipped Chocolate Cookie Sticks

PREP 25 minutes
BAKE 8 minutes   CHILL 1 hour

24 servings	ingredients	48 servings
one 16.5-oz. pkg.	refrigerated chocolate chip cookie dough	two 16.5-oz. pkg.
½ cup	all-purpose flour	1 cup
1 cup	semisweet chocolate pieces	2 cups
1 Tbsp.	shortening	2 Tbsp.

Melting a little bit of shortening with the semisweet chocolate helps ensure that the glaze has a nice, smooth consistency and that it will set up well.

1. Preheat oven to 375°F. In a large bowl combine cookie dough and flour. Shape dough into 1-inch balls and shape balls into 5-inch ropes. Place ropes on an ungreased cookie sheet about 2 inches apart.

2. Bake 8 to 10 minutes or until golden. Cool completely on cookie sheet on a wire rack.

3. In a small saucepan combine chocolate and shortening over low heat. Stir until chocolate is melted and smooth. Dip the sticks in the chocolate mixture and place on a parchment-paper-covered baking sheet. Chill 1 hour or until chocolate is set.

PER SERVING *143 cal., 7 g fat (3 g sat. fat), 1 mg chol., 66 mg sodium, 19 g carb., 1 g fiber, 1 g pro.*

Index

Metric Information

PRODUCT DIFFERENCES

Most of the ingredients called for in the recipes in this book are available in most countries. However, some are known by different names. Here are some common American ingredients and their possible counterparts:

- Sugar (white) is granulated, fine granulated, or castor sugar.
- Powdered sugar is icing sugar.
- All-purpose flour is enriched bleached or unbleached white household flour. When self-rising flour is used in place of all-purpose flour in a recipe that calls for leavening, omit the leavening agent (baking soda or baking powder) and salt.
- Light-color corn syrup is golden syrup.
- Cornstarch is cornflour.
- Baking soda is bicarbonate of soda.
- Vanilla or vanilla extract is vanilla essence.
- Green, red, or yellow sweet peppers are capsicums or bell peppers.
- Golden raisins are sultanas.

VOLUME AND WEIGHT

The United States traditionally uses cup measures for liquid and solid ingredients. The chart (above right) shows the approximate imperial and metric equivalents. If you are accustomed to weighing solid ingredients, the following approximate equivalents will be helpful.

- 1 cup butter, castor sugar, or rice = 8 ounces = ½ pound = 250 grams
- 1 cup flour = 4 ounces = ¼ pound = 125 grams
- 1 cup icing sugar = 5 ounces = 150 grams
- Canadian and U.S. volume for a cup measure is 8 fluid ounces (237 ml), but the standard metric equivalent is 250 ml.
- 1 British imperial cup is 10 fluid ounces.
- In Australia, 1 tablespoon equals 20 ml, and there are 4 teaspoons in the Australian tablespoon.
- Spoon measures are used for small amounts of ingredients. Although the size of the tablespoon varies slightly in different countries, for practical purposes and for recipes in this book, a straight substitution is all that's necessary. Measurements made using cups or spoons always should be level unless stated otherwise.

COMMON WEIGHT RANGE REPLACEMENTS

Imperial / U.S.	Metric
½ ounce	15 g
1 ounce	25 g or 30 g
4 ounces (¼ pound)	115 g or 125 g
8 ounces (½ pound)	225 g or 250 g
16 ounces (1 pound)	450 g or 500 g
1¼ pounds	625 g
1½ pounds	750 g
2 pounds or 2¼ pounds	1,000 g or 1 Kg

OVEN TEMPERATURE EQUIVALENTS

Fahrenheit Setting	Celsius Setting	Gas Setting
300°F	150°C	Gas Mark 2 (very low)
325°F	160°C	Gas Mark 3 (low)
350°F	180°C	Gas Mark 4 (moderate)
375°F	190°C	Gas Mark 5 (moderate)
400°F	200°C	Gas Mark 6 (hot)
425°F	220°C	Gas Mark 7 (hot)
450°F	230°C	Gas Mark 8 (very hot)
475°F	240°C	Gas Mark 9 (very hot)
500°F	260°C	Gas Mark 10 (extremely hot)
Broil	Broil	Grill

*Electric and gas ovens may be calibrated using Celsius. However, for an electric oven, increase Celsius setting 10 to 20 degrees when cooking above 160°C. For convection or forced-air ovens (gas or electric), lower the temperature setting 25°F/10°C when cooking at all heat levels.

BAKING PAN SIZES

Imperial / U.S.	Metric
9×1½-inch round cake pan	22- or 23×4-cm (1.5 L)
9×1½-inch pie plate	22- or 23×4-cm (1 L)
8×8×2-inch square cake pan	20×5-cm (2 L)
9×9×2-inch square cake pan	22- or 23×4.5-cm (2.5 L)
11×7×1½-inch baking pan	28×17×4-cm (2 L)
2-quart rectangular baking pan	30×19×4.5-cm (3 L)
13×9×2-inch baking pan	34×22×4.5-cm (3.5 L)
15×10×1-inch jelly roll pan	40×25×2-cm
9×5×3-inch loaf pan	23×13×8-cm (2 L)
2-quart casserole	2 L

U.S. / STANDARD METRIC EQUIVALENTS

⅛ teaspoon = 0.5 ml	
¼ teaspoon = 1 ml	
½ teaspoon = 2 ml	
1 teaspoon = 5 ml	
1 tablespoon = 15 ml	
2 tablespoons = 25 ml	
¼ cup = 2 fluid ounces = 50 ml	
⅓ cup = 3 fluid ounces = 75 ml	
½ cup = 4 fluid ounces = 125 ml	
⅔ cup = 5 fluid ounces = 150 ml	
¾ cup = 6 fluid ounces = 175 ml	
1 cup = 8 fluid ounces = 250 ml	
2 cups = 1 pint = 500 ml	
1 quart = 1 litre	